Steven Holzner

Sams **Teach Yourself**

Google
SketchUp 8

in **10 Minutes**

800 East 96th Street, Indianapolis, Indiana 46240

Sams Teach Yourself Google SketchUp 8 in 10 Minutes

ISBN-13: 978-0-672-33547-1
ISBN-10: 0-672-33547-6

Library of Congress Cataloging-in-Publication Data:

Holzner, Steven.

Sams teach yourself Google SketchUp 8 in 10 minutes / Steven Holzner.

p. cm.

ISBN-13: 978-0-672-33547-1

ISBN-10: 0-672-33547-6

1. Computer graphics. 2. SketchUp. 3. Three-dimensional display systems. 4. Engineering graphics. I. Title.

T385.H6774 2011

006.6'93—dc22

2010049018

Printed in the United States of America

First Printing January 2011

Trademarks

Warning and Disclaimer

Bulk Sales

Pearson offers excellent discounts on this book when ordered in quantity for bulk purchases or special sales. For more information, please contact

> **U.S. Corporate and Government Sales**
> **1-800-382-3419**
> corpsales@pearsontechgroup.com

For sales outside of the U.S., please contact

> **International Sales**
> international@pearsoned.com

Editor-in-Chief
Greg Wiegand

Acquisitions Editor
Rick Kughen

Development Editor
Mark Reddin

Managing Editor
Sandra Schroeder

Senior Project Editor
Tonya Simpson

Copy Editor
Barbara Hacha

Indexer
Tim Wright

Technical Editor
Todd Meister

Publishing Coordinator
Cindy Teeters

Book Designer
Anne Jones

Compositor
Mark Shirar

Table of Contents

About the Author

Steven Holzner is the award-winning author of more than 100 books, specializing in online topics such as Google Buzz, Gmail, and more. He's been a contributing editor of *PC Magazine* and has specialized in online computing for many years. His books have sold more than 2.5 million copies and have been translated into 18 languages. Steve graduated from MIT and earned his PhD at Cornell. He's been a very popular member of the faculty at both MIT and Cornell, teaching thousands of students over the years. He also runs his own software company and teaches weeklong classes to corporate programmers around the country.

Dedication

To Nancy, of course.

Acknowledgements

The book you hold in your hands is the product of the work of many people. I would especially like to thank Rick Kughen, Mark Reddin, Todd Meister, Tonya Simpson, and Barbara Hacha.

We Want to Hear from You!

As the reader of this book, *you* are our most important critic and commentator. We value your opinion and want to know what we're doing right, what we could do better, what areas you'd like to see us publish in, and any other words of wisdom you're willing to pass our way.

You can email or write me directly to let me know what you did or didn't like about this book—as well as what we can do to make our books stronger.

Please note that I cannot help you with technical problems related to the topic of this book, and that due to the high volume of mail I receive, I might not be able to reply to every message.

When you write, please be sure to include this book's title and author as well as your name and phone or email address. I will carefully review your comments and share them with the author and editors who worked on the book.

E-mail: consumer@samspublishing.com

Mail: Greg Wiegand
          Editor-in-Chief
          Sams Publishing
          800 East 96th Street
          Indianapolis, IN 46240 USA

Reader Services

Visit our website and register this book at informit.com/register for convenient access to any updates, downloads, or errata that might be available for this book.

Introduction

Welcome to SketchUp! This book is all about Google's fantastically popular 3D modeling program, ready for you to create 3D drawings with.

SketchUp is ultrapowerful, and lets you draw models with ease. Need to draw a new engine? SketchUp can do it. Need to lay out your back yard plantings? SketchUp can help. Want to plan a new office, positioning chairs, desks, and workstations as needed? SketchUp is for you.

SketchUp's forte is 3D modeling—creating drawings of 3D objects. There are plenty of 2D drawing programs out there but very few of SketchUp's caliber and ease of use for 3D.

Want to become a SketchUp-meister? Stay tuned, you've come to the right book.

> NOTE: **What's New In Google SketchUp 8**
> SketchUp 8 offers a variety of new features not found in SketchUp 7. For a list of what's new in SketchUp, see http://sketchup.google.com/product/newin8.html

What's in This Book

You're going to get a guided tour of SketchUp in this book. SketchUp is too large a program to cover in complete detail in a book this size, but you're going to get a real working knowledge of SketchUp, suitable for creating just about any drawing you want.

SketchUp offers you a super-powerful set of tools to work with, and this book is about those tools. We'll see how to draw basic figures using tools such as

- ▶ The Rectangle tool
- ▶ The Circle tool

- ▶ The Polygon tool
- ▶ The Arc tool

as well as how to draw freehand.

We'll see how to use tools to convert from 2D to 3D—tools like

- ▶ The Push/Pull tool
- ▶ The Move tool
- ▶ The Rotate tool

After going 3D, we'll make use of the tools SketchUp offers for viewing 3D objects, such as

- ▶ The Orbit tool
- ▶ The Pan tool
- ▶ The Zoom tool

Having mastered 3D concepts and after we're used to creating 3D objects, we'll see how to measure lengths and angles, as well as construct construction guides with tools such as

- ▶ The Tape Measure tool
- ▶ The Dimensioning tool
- ▶ The Protractor tool

Then we'll start getting into some tools specific to SketchUp, giving you more 3D power:

- ▶ The Offset tool
- ▶ The Follow-Me tool
- ▶ The Section Pane tool

And more!

These tools are particular to SketchUp, and only SketchUp offers their kind of power. The Offset tool lets you draw copies of edges at offsets from the original in case you want to repeat that surface (as when, for example, you're drawing an ornate window frame and want to copy a curved edge to create a whole window frame). The Follow-Me tool is an amazing one—it lets you specify a path and a shape or action, then pulls that shape or action around your path, giving you a 3D result (so, for example, if you bevel one side of a chair seat and want to bevel the other three sides similarly, you can use the Follow-Me tool). And the Section Pane tool lets you draw cross-sections through any surface in your model.

And there are yet more tools coming up, such as the Scale tool, which enlarges or reduces models just by dragging the mouse, the Text Annotation tool, which lets you add notes to your models, the 3D Text tool, which lets you draw 3D text, and more.

All of which is to say: there's a lot coming up on your guided tour.

Conventions Used in This Book

Whenever you need to click a particular button or link in SketchUp, you'll find the label or name for that item bolded in the text, such as "click the **Line tool**." In addition to the text and figures in this book, you also encounter some special boxes labelled Tip, Note, or Caution.

> TIP: Tips offer helpful shortcuts or easier ways to do something.

> NOTE: Notes are extra bits of information related to the text that might help you expand your knowledge or understanding.

> CAUTION: Cautions are warnings or other important information you need to know about consequences of using a feature or executing a task.

What You'll Need

All you'll need to use this book is Google SketchUp itself.

SketchUp comes in two versions—free and paid. The paid version is the "professional" version, but the free version is also immensely powerful. We'll be using the free version here. All you have to do is to download and install it, following the directions at the beginning of Lesson 2.

That's it. Everything you need for this book comes in SketchUp itself. There's nothing else needed. After you've installed the free version, you're ready to roll.

LESSON 1

Welcome to SketchUp

Welcome to Google SketchUp—the most powerful 3D graphics program you can get for free (and it even comes in a paid version as well for extra power).

Getting Started with SketchUp

There's a huge amount of material to cover when talking about SketchUp, so we're going to spend this first lesson getting a short overview of what's possible. In the book as a whole, we're going to get a real working knowledge of SketchUp—enough to get you building and working with complex models.

Let's start by taking a look at SketchUp itself, which appears in Figure 1.1.

As you can see in Figure 1.1, Google SketchUp gives you a set of three axes, giving your drawing a 3D feel from the start. That's appropriate because SketchUp is a 3D program; that is its main claim to fame.

It's simple to create 3D objects in SketchUp, and you can do so in a variety of ways, as we're going to see. The most amazing 3D models are possible in SketchUp. Take a look at Figure 1.2, for example.

You draw models like the one in the figure using tools from the toolbars. By selecting individual tools such as the Line tool, the Circle tool, the Polygon tool, and so on, you create the shapes step by step that compose your desired model.

Let's start with an overview of SketchUp in this lesson; then we'll install and start working with SketchUp in the next lesson.

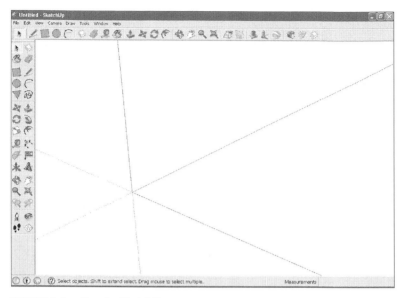

FIGURE 1.1   Google SketchUp.

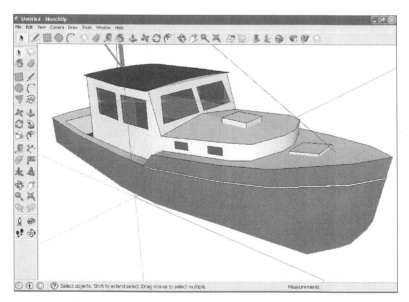

FIGURE 1.2   A 3D model.

Drawing Lines

When you first start SketchUp, the Line tool is selected by default. And, as you might expect, you can draw lines with this tool—see Figure 1.3.

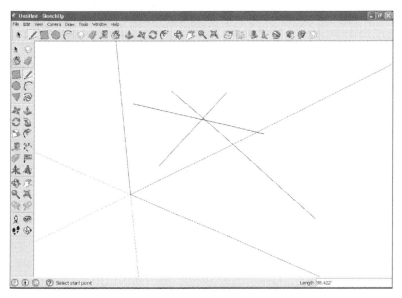

FIGURE 1.3   Drawing lines.

Drawing lines is one of the simplest of figures you can make in SketchUp—lines are one-dimensional, so they don't exhibit any of the helpful behavior SketchUp adds to other figures, such as snapping to axes, being colored automatically, and more, as we're about to see.

Drawing Simple Figures

Using tools such as the Rectangle tool, you can draw 2D shapes, like the rectangle you see in Figure 1.4.

Besides rectangles, you can draw circles, polygons, and arcs using the corresponding tools.

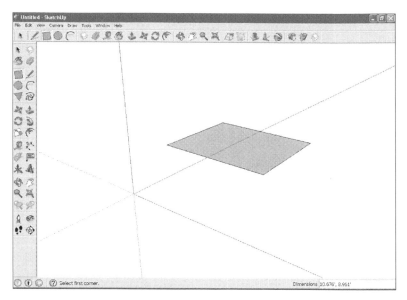

FIGURE 1.4   A horizontal rectangle.

> NOTE: **Starting Simple**
>
> Information about the various tools is spread across all the lessons in this book; you are encouraged to follow them in order because they build on one another. However, you'll find specific coverage in certain lessons. For example, there's more on drawing lines, rectangles, and other simple figures in Lesson 3, "Drawing Shapes: Lines, Rectangles, Polygons, and Circles."

Notice that the rectangle in Figure 1.4 has an orientation—it's horizontal. Keep in mind that Google SketchUp is a 3D program. When you draw a 2D figure, you're drawing a 2D figure in 3D.

By default, SketchUp makes such a figure horizontal, although you can rotate it. SketchUp will also snap 2D figures to any underlying surface, aligning them along that surface, as you can see in Figure 1.5, where we've drawn rectangles that SketchUp has snapped to the sides of a 3D polygon.

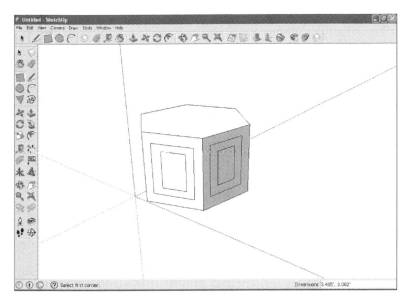

FIGURE 1.5   Rectangles snapped to the sides of a 3D polygon.

How do we create a 3D object like the one in Figure 1.5? By going 3D, as we'll see in the next section.

Pushing (or Pulling) for 3D

Converting objects from 2D to 3D in SketchUp is one of the coolest things you can do. How does it work? You draw a 2D shape, and then pull (or push) it into 3D.

For example, take a look at the polygon shape shown previously in Figure 1.5, the one with the rectangles on its sides. SketchUp recognizes the rectangles as shapes, and so lets you pull them into 3D from the surrounding surface using such tools as the Push/Pull tool.

For example, using the Push/Pull tool, you can push in the inner rectangle in each face of the object, as you see in Figure 1.6.

All you do is select the Push/Pull tool, press the mouse button on the shape you want to push or pull into 3D, and, holding the mouse button

down, push or pull the shape. It'll be pushed into or pulled out of the surrounding surface, as you see in Figure 1.6.

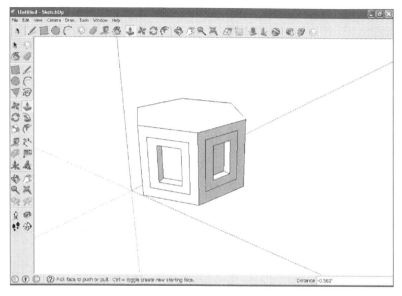

FIGURE 1.6   A 3D object.

You can the elaborate the object by pulling out the larger rectangles into
3D, as you see in Figure 1.7.

A couple more clicks let you add more structure to the object, as you see
in Figure 1.8.

Using the Push/Pull tool, you can also cut out sections of existing objects
to create holes, or windows, in those objects, as you see in Figure 1.9.

Panning and Orbiting

Given that objects exist in 3D in SketchUp, you might think that there are
various tools that let you see objects from various perspectives, and you'd
be right.

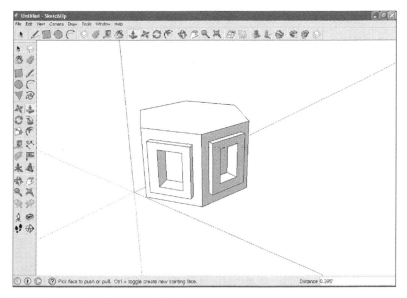

FIGURE 1.7   An elaborated 3D object.

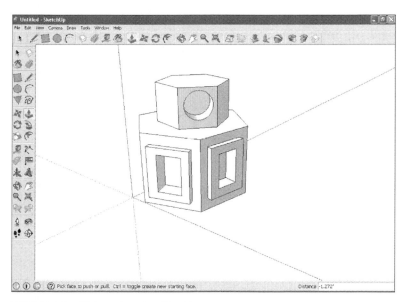

FIGURE 1.8   Elaborating the 3D object even more.

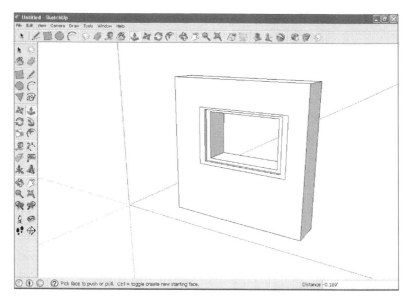

FIGURE 1.9   A window.

Creating and manipulating 3D models is something you'll likely spend a lot of time doing in SketchUp. We'll get deeper into using the Push/Pull tool in Lesson 5, "Going 3D."

For example, you can use the Pan tool to move the drawing left or right, up or down, or any combination of these, as you see in Figures 1.10 and 1.11.

You can also use the Orbit tool for a more truly 3D experience. This tool lets you "orbit" around a model, changing perspective to any angle, as you can see in Figures 1.12 and 1.13.

> NOTE: **Want More?**
> Panning and orbiting are given the in-depth treatment in Lesson 2, "Up and Running with SketchUp."

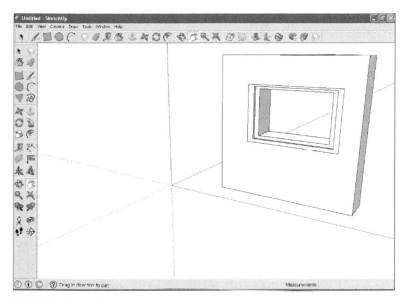

FIGURE 1.10 Panning a drawing one way.

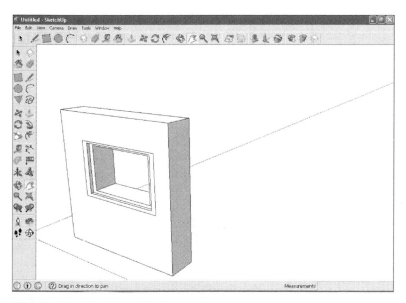

FIGURE 1.11 Panning a drawing another way.

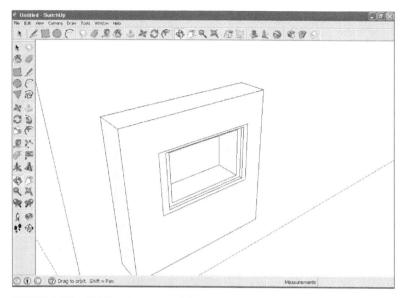

FIGURE 1.12   Orbiting to one position.

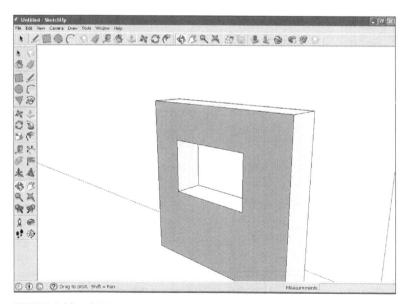

FIGURE 1.13   Orbiting to another position.

You can also move and rotate objects themselves rather than just perspective.

Rotating and Moving

Although these tools are fairly self-explanatory, they are incredibly useful, as you might imagine. Note that while the Orbit tool lets you orbit around an object, the Rotate tool lets you rotate the object itself.

Take a look at Figure 1.14, showing a piano and a drum set.

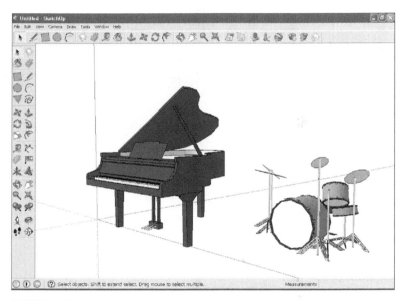

FIGURE 1.14   A piano and a drum set.

Using the Rotate tool, you can rotate objects, as shown in Figure 1.15.

And using the Move tool, you can move objects around your drawing, as shown in Figure 1.16. Notice that the piano has been rotated from its position shown in Figure 1.15.

There is an infinite number of reasons you might want to rotate or move objects, so for more on these tools check out Lesson 8, "Using the Rotate, Scale, and Follow-Me Tools," and Lesson 5, "Going 3D," respectively.

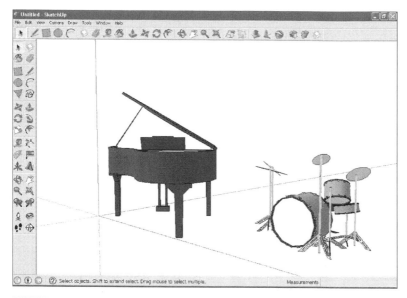

FIGURE 1.15   Rotating an object.

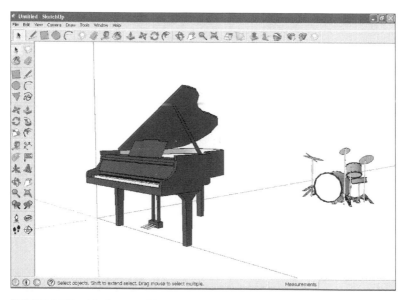

FIGURE 1.16   Moving an object.

Painting

Google SketchUp lets you paint the objects you create. You can paint them with solid colors, and you can select from dozens of textures as well.

For example, say you want to draw three wooden crates. You draw three cubes as shown in Figure 1.17, but they don't look much like wooden crates.

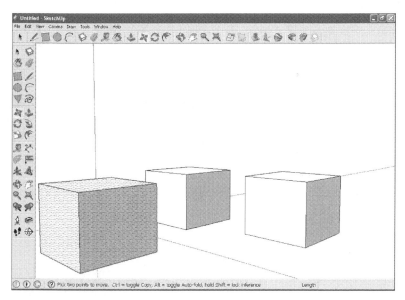

FIGURE 1.17   Three cubes.

Using the Paint tool and selecting a texture, you can paint them to look like wooden crates with a few clicks, as you can see in Figure 1.18 (in black in white in this book, of course).

SketchUp provides the board-by-board texture and aligns the boards to the various surfaces automatically. All you have to do is click a surface to paint on. You'll learn more about painting in Lesson 7, "Painting Your Objects."

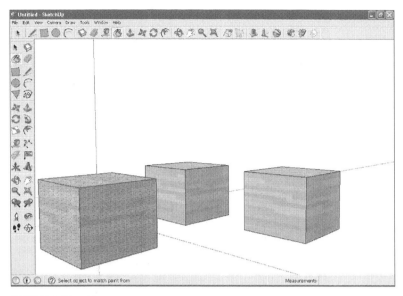

FIGURE 1.18   Three crates.

Using the Component Libraries

Google maintains a 3D warehouse of prebuilt models for you to download and use. There are dozens of such prebuilt models, and using them can save you plenty of time.

Models with multiple parts are treated as a single unit called *components* in SketchUp, and SketchUp offers you a number of component collections in its 3D warehouse:

- ▶ Architecture
- ▶ Landscape
- ▶ Construction
- ▶ People
- ▶ Playground
- ▶ Transportation

Inside each collection are multiple subcategories. For example, you can
see the subcategories for the Architecture category in Figure 1.19.

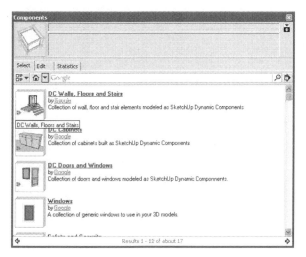

FIGURE 1.19   The Architecture subcategories.

Some subcategories are themselves divided into further subcategories—for
example, the Furniture collection in the Architecture collection is divided
into the collections you can see in Figure 1.20.

You can see actual models from the furniture collection in Figure 1.21.

And you can see a simple glass-topped table from the collection in
Figure 1.22.

As you can see, there are dozens of models waiting for you to use them.
We'll get more in-depth with these in Lesson 6, "Creating Components
and Groups."

Zooming

Another powerful tool is the Zoom tool, which lets you zoom in and out.
For example, suppose you have the drawing in Figure 1.23, a small boat,
and you want a closer look.

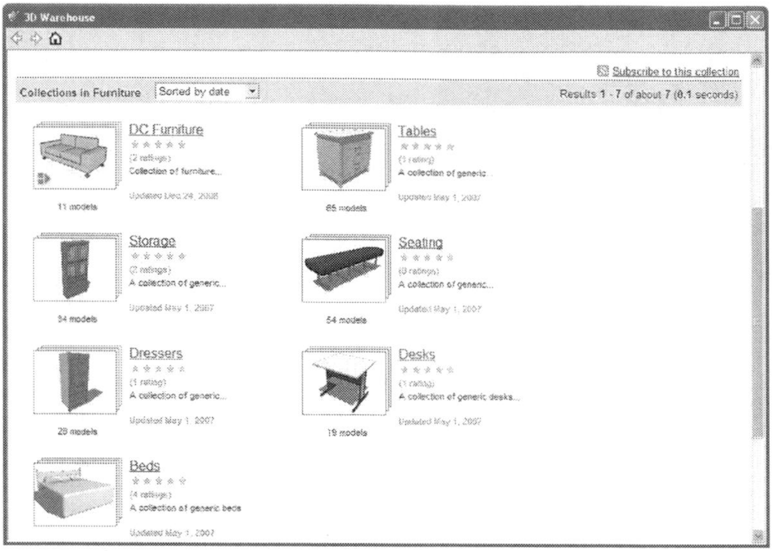

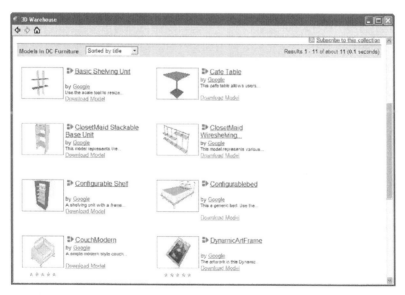

FIGURE 1.20   The Furniture subcategories.

FIGURE 1.21   Furniture models.

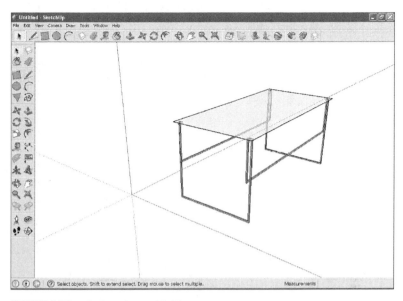

FIGURE 1.22   A glass-topped table.

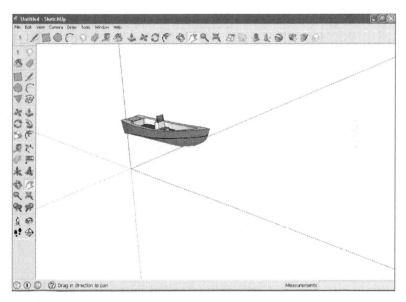

FIGURE 1.23   A small boat.

You can zoom in with the Zoom tool to see more detail, as you can see in Figure 1.24.

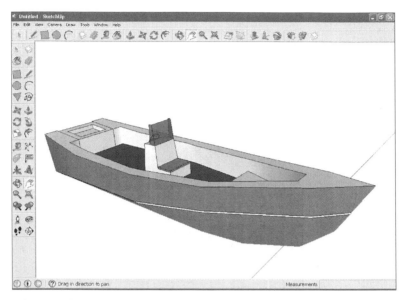

FIGURE 1.24   Zooming in on a small boat.

In fact, zooming is such a common thing to do in SketchUp that the mouse wheel is reserved for this purpose—wheeling one way zooms in, the other zooms out.

Creating Guides and Dimension Indicators

There are all kinds of construction aids in SketchUp as well. For example, take a look at Figure 1.25, where you can see a cube with some construction guides added.

Construction guides can be positioned anywhere in a drawing, and you can use them to align objects. As you can see, they appear as dotted lines in a drawing, and if you wanted to add another cube lined up with the current one, you could use those guides to help.

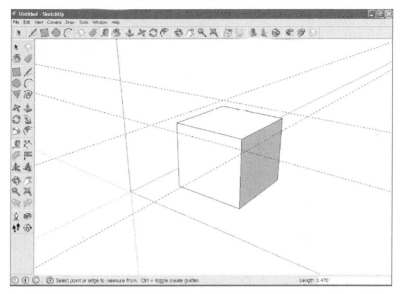

FIGURE 1.25   A cube with construction guides.

You can also add dimensioning indicators to a drawing, as you see in Figure 1.26.

Those dimensions will change as you resize an object. Lesson 10, "Dimensioning, Drawing Angles, and Getting Cross Sections of Models" is where you will find more on this topic.

Lots of Cool Stuff Coming Up

There is a lot of cool stuff coming up, such as the Follow-Me tool, which lets you specify a path and a shape, as you see in Figure 1.27.

With the Follow-Me tool, you can make SketchUp move the shape along the path you've specified, resulting in a new object, as you see in Figure 1.28.

Suppose you had a model of a playground, as shown in Figure 1.29.

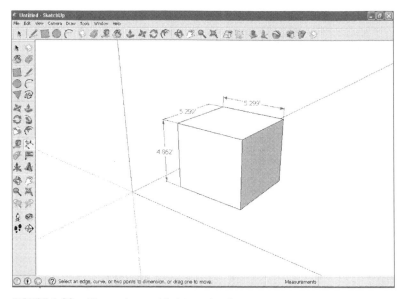

FIGURE 1.26   Dimensions added to a drawing.

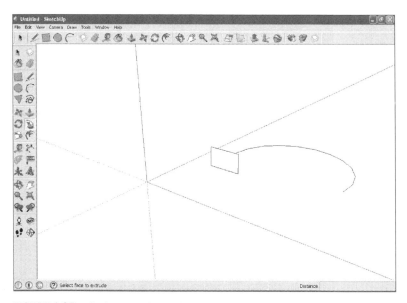

FIGURE 1.27   A shape and a path.

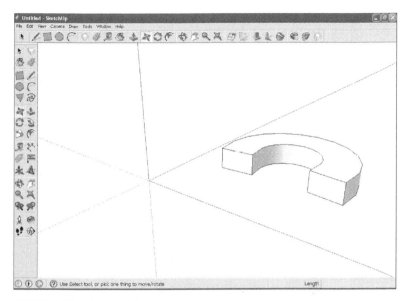

FIGURE 1.28   A new object.

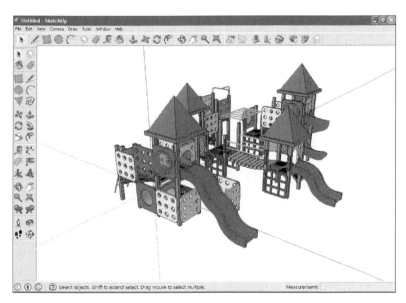

FIGURE 1.29   A playground.

You can take a cross section of the model anywhere you want to get a clearer view of various components, as you see in Figure 1.30.

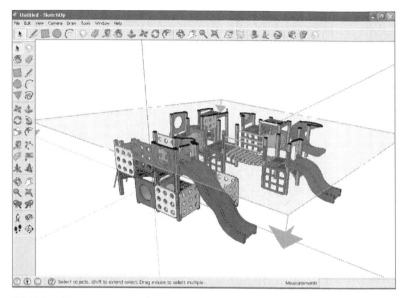

FIGURE 1.30   A sectioned playground.

You can even do 3D text, as you see in Figure 1.31.

With all this coming up, let's dig in immediately to the next lesson and get you up and running with SketchUp!

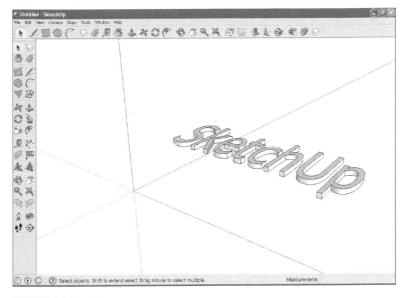

FIGURE 1.31 3D text.

Up and Running with SketchUp

You're about to start working with an amazing program—Google SketchUp.

What SketchUp Is All About

The name of the game with Google SketchUp is 3D drawing. Not just drawing, because there are tons of programs out there to help you with that, but 3D drawing. In this lesson, you'll see how easy and quick it is to create 3D drawings.

That's not to say that all of SketchUp is easy. A program this complex has some sticky points, which we're going to cover in this book. But Google has made 3D drawing just about as simple as it could become and still retain real power.

SketchUp comes in two versions—SketchUp itself, which is free, and SketchUp Pro, which is not. We're going to be using SketchUp—the free version—in this book, but you should also know SketchUp Pro is available in case SketchUp doesn't meet your needs.

> **TIP: SketchUp Pro**
>
> SketchUp Pro is 3D modeling software for professionals. Pro is billed as being everything that traditional CAD software is, only easier to learn and more intuitive. Pro enables you to import drawings, CAD plans, photos, aerial imagery, and more. It also enables you to export and share your projects more easily. At $495, however, Pro is a significant investment. We recommend that you give the free

version a try first. It might do everything you need and more.
However, if you use SketchUp extensively and need the more powerful features offered in the Pro edition, you might consider ponying
up for the upgrade. Go to the following site to compare features in
Pro with the features found in the free version: http://sketchup.
google.com/intl/en/product/whygopro.html

This lesson gets us started with SketchUp. We'll see where to get it and
install it. Then we'll start SketchUp and cover the basic concepts you need
to know before using it.

Then we'll take it out for a spin.

Let's jump in immediately by installing SketchUp.

Getting and Installing SketchUp

You can download SketchUp for free from its website. Just follow these
directions:

1. Navigate to the SketchUp site, www.sketchup.com (or http:/
   /sketchup.google.com). The SketchUp site appears, as shown in
   Figure 2.1.

2. Click the **Download Google SketchUp** button. This causes the
   page you see in Figure 2.2 to appear.

3. Click the **Download Google SketchUp** button again. This brings
   up the license agreement you see in Figure 2.3.

4. Select the option button for your operating system. The choices are

   ▶ Windows XP/Vista/7

   ▶ Mac OS X (10.5+)

5. Read the terms and click the **Agree and Download** button.

6. Let your browser download and save the installation file.
   Depending on your browser, you might have to click a yellow bar
   at top of the browser window and select the **Download File**
   menu item. If your browser asks you where to save the file, select
   a convenient directory, or create a new one named SketchUp.

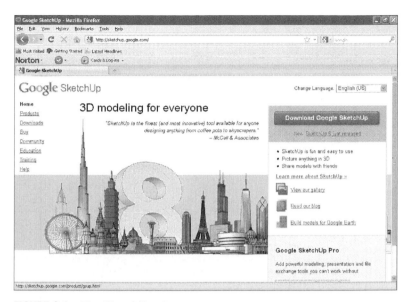

FIGURE 2.1 The SketchUp site.

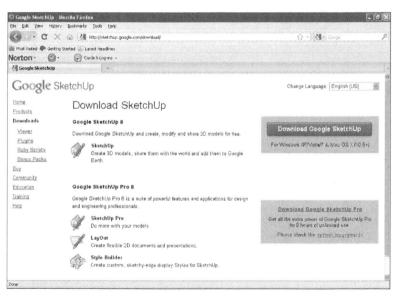

FIGURE 2.2 The second page of the download process.

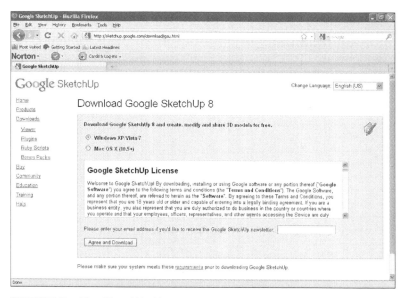

FIGURE 2.3   The SketchUp License agreement page.

7. Double-click the downloaded file. A dialog box may appear warning you of the risk of running downloaded files. If so, click the **Run** button in the dialog box. The SketchUp installer starts, as shown in Figure 2.4.

8. Click the **Next** button. SketchUp displays agreement text for you to read.

9. If you agree, select the I Agree to the Terms of the License Agreement check box.

10. Click **Next**.

11. SketchUp displays a dialog box displaying its preferred default location on your disk. If you want to change the installation location from the default, click the **Change** button and enter the new installation directory, then click **OK**.

12. Click **Next**.

13. Click **Install** to begin the installation. Google SketchUp is installed, and a final dialog box appears.

FIGURE 2.4   The SketchUp Setup Wizard.

14. Click **Finish**.

That's it—you've installed Google SketchUp.

Starting SketchUp

Let's fire up SketchUp and see what we've downloaded. After getting it started in this task, we'll get used to a few essential tools in the following task.

1. Double-click the **SketchUp** program file to start it, or, in Windows, select it from the Start menu. The dialog box you see in Figure 2.5 appears.

2. Click the **Choose Template** button. The template you select will determine the drawing background (if any) and the units of the drawing (feet, meters, and so on). You need to select a template before SketchUp will start, and the template you choose will become your default template the next time you open SketchUp. When you click the **Choose Template** button, a list of templates appears, as shown in Figure 2.6.

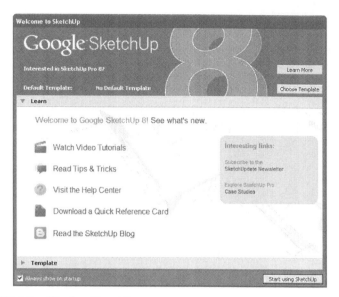

FIGURE 2.5   Starting SketchUp.

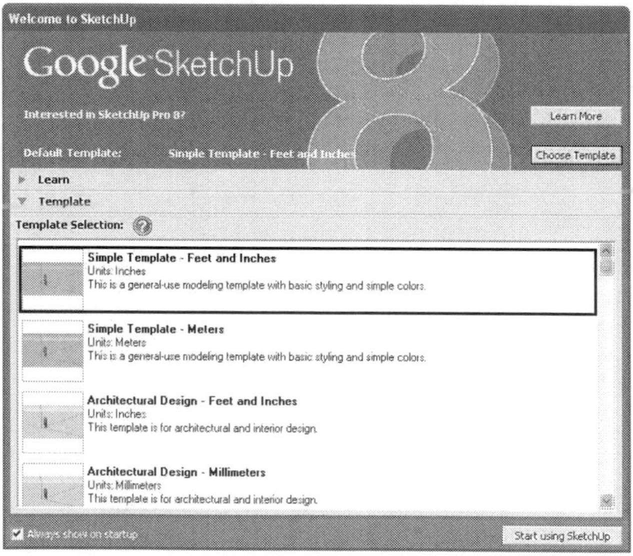

FIGURE 2.6   Selecting a template.

NOTE: **Changing the Default Template**

Selecting a template makes it the default when SketchUp starts up, so when you start SketchUp from now on and click the Start Using SketchUp button, you'll be using the Simple Template selected in step 3. To change that, click the **Choose Template** button and select the template you want, then click the **Start Using SketchUp** button.

3. Click the top template to select it, as shown in Figure 2.6. We'll use other templates in the following lessons, but the Simple template gives us a blue sky, green Earth, and a person standing in the middle for scale—a good template to get started with.

4. Click the **Start Using SketchUp** button. SketchUp appears, as shown in Figure 2.7, using the template we've selected as background.

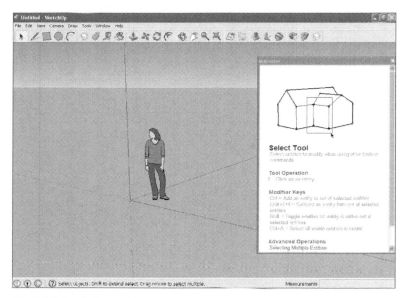

FIGURE 2.7   A Simple Template in Google SketchUp.

Now you've got SketchUp running—congratulations.

NOTE: **Listen to the Instructor**

Note the dialog box along the right side, showing information about the Select tool. This dialog box is called the Instructor, and it's very useful to learn about the tools in the toolbox, which appear at the top of the SketchUp window. The Select tool (an arrow much like the default mouse pointer) is the default tool in SketchUp, active when you start SketchUp, which is why the Instructor is explaining its use in selecting items in SketchUp.

Leave the Instructor open for now because it's a very useful guide to the tools in the toolbox. When you close the Instructor later, you can get it back by clicking the round question mark button at the bottom of SketchUp.

Understanding the Parts of SketchUp

As with most applications, you need to become familiar with the basic elements. Let's take a look at the various parts of SketchUp, as shown in Figure 2.8.

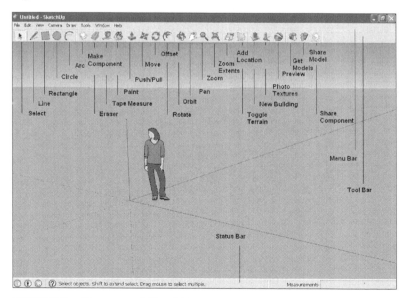

FIGURE 2.8   The parts of SketchUp.

As you'd expect, SketchUp comes with the normal parts of most applications you're familiar with:

▶ **The menu bar**—Includes familiar menus such as File, Edit, and so on. We'll be making use of the items in SketchUp's menus throughout this book.

NOTE: **The Getting Started Toolbars**

Note that by default, SketchUp shows only its Getting Started toolbar, which is the toolbar you see in Figure 2.8. To see the full tool set, select the **View** menu, then the **Toolbars** item, then the **Large Tool Set** menu item.

▶ **The toolbar**—Includes various drawing tools, as you can see labeled in Figure 2.8.

▶ **The status bar**—Contains buttons to show you who designed the current item open in SketchUp, information about the current item, and a Help button (the button with the question mark caption) that turns the Instructor dialog box on and off.

That's SketchUp in overview. Now let's start using some tools.

Using the Orbit Tool

There are three primary tools that you have to get familiar with to start working with SketchUp: Orbit, Pan, and Zoom. We'll take a look at the Orbit tool in this task and the Pan and Zoom tools in the following two tasks.

The reason that these three tools are the important ones to start out with is that they give you a handle on working in 2D. New users not familiar with these tools can grope around in the dark in SketchUp before finally getting a grip on how to work with 3D.

The Orbit tool lets you examine a 2D figure—called a *model* in SketchUp—from all different directions. By rotating the Orbit tool, you can examine the model you're creating from all angles.

Here's how to use the Orbit tool:

1. Start SketchUp. The Welcome to SketchUp dialog box appears. For this task, we'll work with the Simple Template we've used in the previous tasks.

2. Click the **Start Using SketchUp** button. This opens SketchUp using the Simple Template from the previous task as the default template, as shown in Figure 2.9.

The Orbit Tool

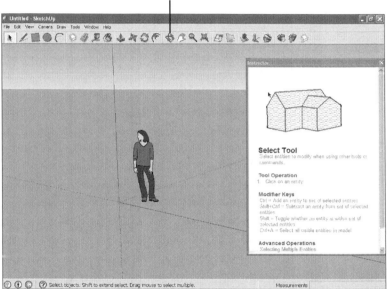

FIGURE 2.9   Starting SketchUp and selecting the Orbit tool.

3. Click the **Orbit** tool in the toolbar (as shown in Figure 2.9).

4. Move the Orbit tool around SketchUp's workspace. As you do, the angle from which you view the current contents of the window changes, as you can see in Figure 2.10. The Orbit tool enables you to view your models in 3D just by moving the tool around the screen.

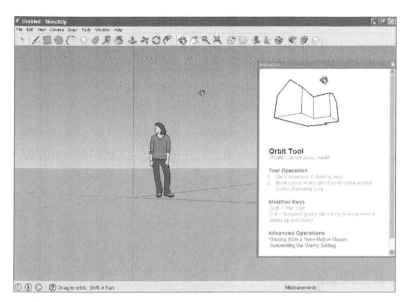

FIGURE 2.10   Using the Orbit tool.

TIP: **Experiment with the Orbit Tool**

It's a good idea to play with the Orbit tool for a while, getting used to what it does, and noting the 3D feeling you get by rotating the current model.

Using the Pan Tool

The Pan tool lets you move from side to side and up and down. The Pan tool's icon is a hand, and that's appropriate, because you "grasp" the display and move it around.

The angle doesn't change when you use the Pan tool, unlike when you use the Orbit tool. Here's how to put the Pan tool to work:

1. Click the **Start Using SketchUp** button. This opens SketchUp with the Simple Template we've set as the default in the previous tasks.

2. Click the **Pan** tool in the toolbar (shown in Figure 2.11).

The Pan Tool

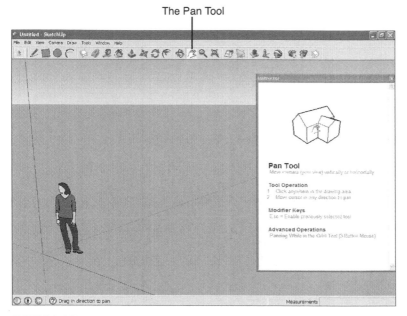

FIGURE 2.11   Using the Pan tool.

3. Press the mouse button in SketchUp's display to "grasp" the display.

4. Drag the mouse to move the display. When you do, the whole display moves around without changing angle or perspective, as you can see in Figure 2.11.

The Pan tool gives you a way of viewing your models by moving them from side to side and up and down.

Using the Zoom Tool

The Zoom tool lets you zoom in and out of the display—that is, magnify your view, if you want to. That's great to see the smaller details of a model.

Here's how to put the Zoom tool to work:

1. Click the **Start Using SketchUp** button. This opens SketchUp with the Simple Template we've set as the default in the previous tasks.

2. Click the **Zoom** tool in the toolbar (shown in Figure 2.12).

The Zoom Tool

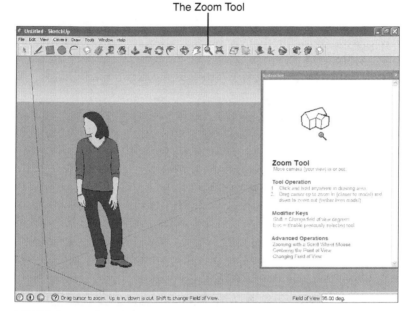

FIGURE 2.12   Using the Zoom tool.

3. Press the mouse button in SketchUp's display.

4. Drag the mouse upward to zoom the display in and drag downward to zoom the display out. When you do, the whole display zooms in and out without changing angle or perspective, as you can see in Figure 2.12.

The Zoom tool gives you a way of magnifying your models—very handy at times.

> TIP: **Using the Mouse Wheel to Zoom**
> If your mouse has a wheel on it, you can zoom in and out just by thumbing the wheel—even if a tool such as the Select tool is selected and not the Zoom tool.

Selecting a Work Template

Until now, we've been using the first template that SketchUp had to offer—the Simple Template measured in feet and inches, with a human figure in the middle of it, along with blue sky and green earth.

However, you probably don't want someone standing there in a field under a blue sky when drawing your own models. The most common template to use has no background at all, no sky, no ground—just a set of three axes to show you the three dimensions.

In this task, we see how to select a good working template that has no features other than the three axes. Here's how to set this up:

1. From the Welcome to SketchUp page, click the **Choose Template** button. The template selection dialog box appears.

2. Click the **Engineering–Feet** template to select it (as shown in Figure 2.13).

3. Click the **Start Using SketchUp** button. This opens SketchUp with the Engineering–Feet template.

4. Select the human figure in the template by clicking it. You can see the human figure selected in Figure 2.14.

5. Delete the human figure by pressing the Del key. The figure disappears. You now have a clean slate for creating your own models without any distracting backgrounds.

The Engineering–Feet or Engineering–Meters templates are useful because they don't give you a background, so you're free to design your own. We'll use these templates frequently in this book.

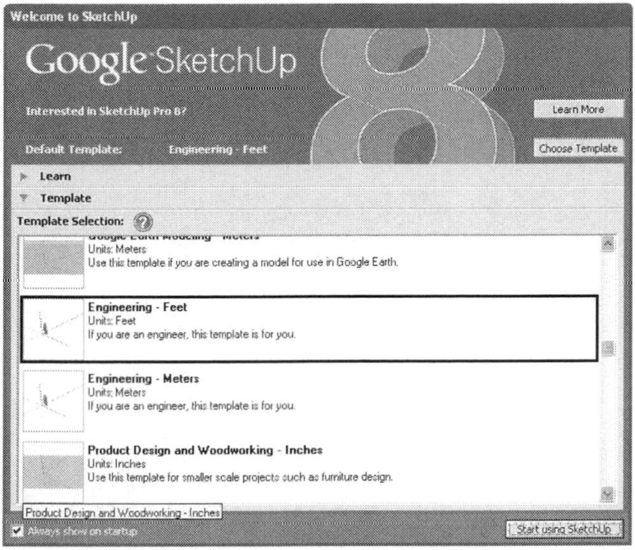

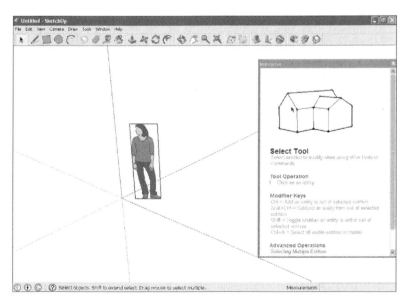

FIGURE 2.13 Selecting the Engineering–Feet template.

FIGURE 2.14 Selecting the human figure.

Understanding SketchUp Axes

If you take a look at Figure 2.14, you'll see three axes corresponding to the x, y, and z axes you may be familiar with. The x and y axes form the horizontal plane, and the z axis points vertically out of that plane.

We'll call the axis in the foreground that's closest to a horizontal line the x axis; the other horizontal axis, which goes into the page, the y axis; and the vertical axis the z axis, as shown in Figure 2.15.

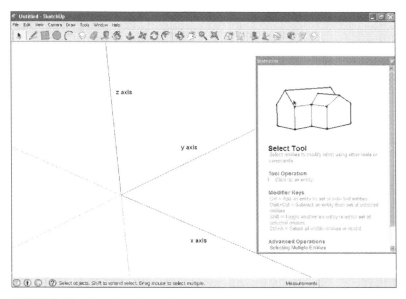

FIGURE 2.15   The three (x, y, z) axes.

Those are the three names we'll use for the axes—x, y, and z.

What you can't see in Figure 2.15 (because this is a black-and-white book) is that the axes are *colored*:

▶ The x axis is red.

▶ The y axis is green.

▶ The z axis is blue.

> TIP: **Axes Coloring**
>
> You'll sometimes see axes referred to by color in the SketchUp help files, so it can be helpful to bear the previous list of color associations in mind.

The reason the axes are colored is that the shapes you draw (see the next lesson) are usually aligned with one or another axis by SketchUp automatically, and SketchUp will indicate the color axis the shape is being aligned with. So, for example, as you draw one edge of a rectangle, a ToolTip (a small yellow window with some text) will appear, reading On Red Axis to show that your drawing action is being aligned with the x (red) axis. This is helpful because by default SketchUp automatically snaps what you draw to be parallel to an axis to let you draw shapes easily without wondering how they will line up with the axes. This will become more apparent as we start to draw shapes in coming sections.

Understanding Edges and Surfaces

Another crucial SketchUp concept is about *edges* and *surfaces*. All models are constructed using edges and surfaces in SketchUp. Edges and surfaces are just what you think they are, as shown in Figure 2.16.

Surfaces are always bounded by edges, and you need a closed figure created out of edges to create a surface. For example, you might use the Line tool to draw two lines, as shown in Figure 2.17.

When you connect the two lines with a third line to create a closed figure, SketchUp automatically recognizes that you've created a surface and colors it in, as shown in Figure 2.18.

> TIP: **Erase an Edge and Your Surface Is Gone**
>
> If you erase one of the bounding edges of a surface, that surface disappears—it's no longer a surface. You can, however, re-create the surface by redrawing the last edge—a process known as *healing* a surface.

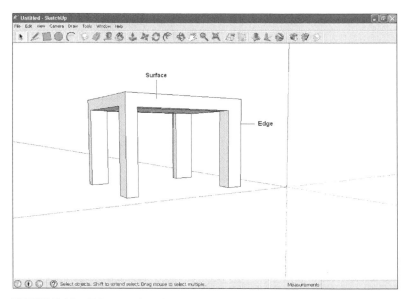

FIGURE 2.16   Edges and surfaces.

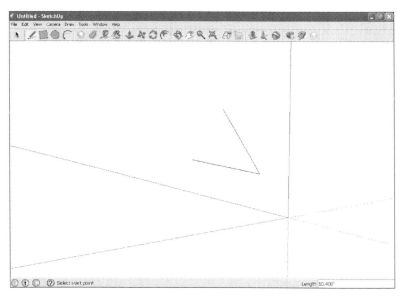

FIGURE 2.17   Two lines.

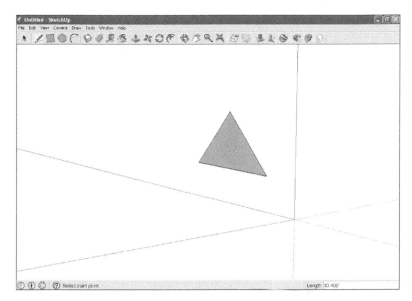

FIGURE 2.18   SketchUp colors in closed figures.

Another thing to know is that a surface must lie in the same plane in
SketchUp. That is, you can't have single surfaces that curl up in any
way—they must be flat. That's not a problem when drawing curved models, however—you simply use a lot of flat surfaces.

TIP: **When a Closed Figure Does Not Create a Surface**

You create surfaces from figures with closed edges, and SketchUp
colors the surface in when it's done. But what happens if you draw
a surface and SketchUp doesn't treat it as a surface and doesn't
color it in as a surface? Often the problem is that the edges you
drew turn out not to be in the same plane. Because SketchUp
snaps the lines you draw to the various axes or other already-drawn
edges, and you're drawing in 3D, it's easy to create figures that are
all in one plane by mistake. However, it's hard to see that they're
not in the same plane. To check whether a surface is all in the
same plane, use the Orbit tool to orbit around it in 3D.

When you draw an edge, by default that edge is aligned with the x, y, or z axis as you draw, and the color of the edge will match the color of the axis (x=red, y=green, z=blue). If you don't want to align a line with the axis SketchUp has chosen, just shift the line as you draw it (by dragging the mouse while you're drawing the line) to match the axis you want, and SketchUp will align the line with that axis.

Drawing Edges

Let's get started doing some actual drawing in SketchUp by drawing a few edges using the Line tool. Here's how it works:

1. Click the **Start Using SketchUp** button. SketchUp starts with the Engineering –Feet template we selected as the default in previous tasks. Click the human figure that appears in the template to select it, and press the Del key to delete it.

2. Click the **Line tool** to select it (shown in Figure 2.19).

3. Press the mouse button where you want one end of the line to start. Pressing the mouse button anchors the line you're about to create.

4. Drag the mouse to the other end of the line. You can see a line being drawn in Figure 2.19.

> **NOTE: SketchUp Automatically Aligns Your Lines**
>
> Note that SketchUp automatically aligns your line with one of the axes (the one you're dragging parallel to) so it's easy to draw exactly parallel to an axis. The line is colored to match the axis it's aligned to (x=red, y=green, z=blue). A ToolTip will appear as you're dragging the mouse to tell you what axis you're aligned with (as appears in Figure 2.19).

The Line
Tool

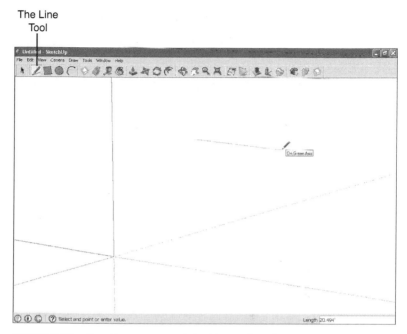

FIGURE 2.19   Use the mouse and the Line tool to draw.

5. Release the mouse button to complete the line. When you release
the mouse button, your new line is drawn and becomes an edge.

Congratulations—you've created a new edge.

To make it easy to draw other edges that connect to this edge, SketchUp
labels various points on the edge as you let the Line tool roll over the
edge, as you can see in Figure 2.20.

TIP: **Connecting Edges**

When you draw an edge that you want to connect to another edge,
you typically let the mouse hover over an end point of the first edge
until the end point circle and the ToolTip labeled Endpoint appears.
Press the mouse button over the end point and then draw the next
edge.

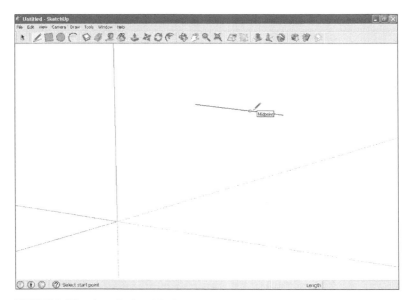

FIGURE 2.20   An edge's midpoint.

In particular, when you hover the Line tool over the ends of an edge (that is, over the line's end points), a small circle appears on the end point of the edge with the ToolTip labeled Endpoint. When you move the Line tool so that it's on the edge (and thus any edge you draw will be connected to the current one), a small red square appears where the mouse cursor is on the line with the ToolTip labeled On Edge. When you hover the Line tool above the midpoint of the edge, a small circle appears on the edge at the location of the mouse pointer with the ToolTip labeled Midpoint (as shown in Figure 2.20).

Inferring Edges

Many times when you're drawing edges, you want to draw one edge parallel to another and end so you can connect the two edges with another edge that goes from end point to end point while the new edge is parallel to an axis. For example, take a look at the situation in Figure 2.21.

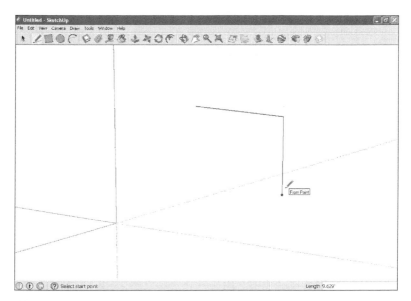

FIGURE 2.21 The need for inferring an edge.

There are two edges there—now suppose you want to draw a third edge on your way to making a rectangle. The third edge will be at the bottom of the figure, parallel to the top edge.

But how far should you draw the bottom edge so that its end point will be directly under the corresponding end point of the top edge? You can guess visually where to stop drawing the third edge so that its end point will end up right under the top edge's end point, but SketchUp provides you with a better way.

Because this is such a common operation—ending an edge at the correct location to match another edge's end point—SketchUp has a special name for it: *inferring*. When you infer an edge, you align it with another edge so that its end point is ready to be connected to another edge's end point with a new edge that is parallel to an axis.

Here's how inferring works, making it easy to draw figures so that all edges line up with axes:

1. Click the **Start Using SketchUp** button. SketchUp starts with the Engineering–Feet template we selected as the default in previous tasks. Click the human figure that appears in the template to select it, and press the Del key to delete it.

2. Click the **Line tool** to select it.

3. Draw two edges like those in Figure 2.21.

4. Draw a new edge from the end point of the vertical edge until a dotted line appears connecting the new edge and the top edge, as shown in Figure 2.22. That dotted line appears automatically as SketchUp infers you might want to line up the current edge's end point with the end point of the top edge.

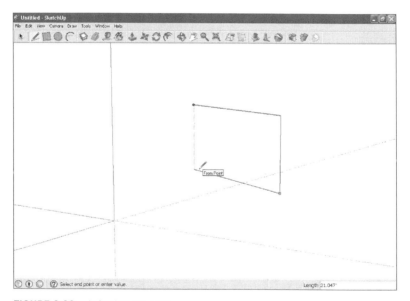

FIGURE 2.22   Inferring an edge.

5. If no dotted line appears, indicate to SketchUp which edge you want it to infer from by letting the mouse pointer hover over the

top edge for two seconds. This establishes which edge you want to infer from, in case SketchUp doesn't guess right. After letting the mouse hover over the edge you want to infer from for two seconds, redraw the third edge, and the dotted line connecting the end points should appear.

6. Release the mouse button to draw the third edge, as shown in Figure 2.23.

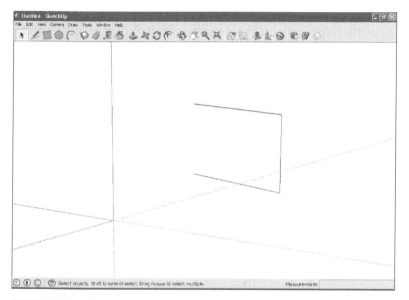

FIGURE 2.23 A new edge.

Now you're in a good position to complete the figure and create a surface (because all edges are in the same plane). To complete the surface, just connect the end points of the top and bottom edges—thanks to inferring, their end points are already lined up.

When you connect the last two end points, SketchUp realizes you've created a surface and colors it in as a surface, as you can see in Figure 2.24.

In the next lesson, we'll start drawing shapes in SketchUp.

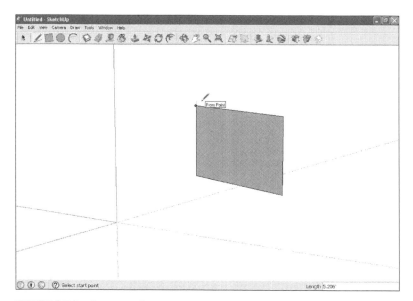

FIGURE 2.24   A new surface.

Drawing Shapes: Lines, Rectangles, Polygons, and Circles

In this lesson, you'll see how to create shapes—rectangles, circles, arcs, and so on. Those are the basic shapes you create other shapes from in SketchUp, and learning how to handle each of these is important.

Getting Started

Bear in mind that what you learned about edges and surfaces in the previous lesson applies here. In particular, it's important to make sure that you don't draw any edge over any other edge.

TIP: **Crossing Edges**

If it looks like you have to draw figures that cross edges, such as a line going across a rectangle, don't. Instead, draw the line up to the rectangle's edge, then draw a new line inside the rectangle to continue. Always remember: don't cross edges, because it confuses SketchUp. We'll see when you can bend this rule later.

Let's jump in immediately by drawing some lines (that is, edges).

TIP: **Selecting a Template**

In this and the following lessons, we're going to be using the Engineering template in SketchUp so that we have no background to get in the way. You're free to select your own template, of course (see Lesson 2, "Up and Running with SketchUp"), but the

---

> Engineering background gives you a clean, empty canvas without any distracting background, so it's recommended when you're just starting out in SketchUp.

Drawing Lines

You use the Line tool in SketchUp to draw—edges. Perhaps you thought I was going to say lines, but in fact, the Line tool really draws edges. You can connect those edges when you draw them, creating a closed figure, which, if it all lies in the same plane, SketchUp treats as a figure.

> TIP: **Drawing Edges**
>
> We already have put the Line tool to work drawing a few edges and closing the figure to complete a surface. Take a look at the previous lesson if you want to bone up on edges and surfaces.

Here's how to use the Line tool to draw an individual edge:

1. Click the **Start Using SketchUp** button on the Welcome page.

2. Click the human figure that appears in the Engineering–Feet template by default to select it and press the Del key to delete it.

3. Click the **Line tool** in the toolbar.

4. Move the mouse to the start point of the new edge you're about to draw.

5. Press the mouse button. Doing so anchors the edge you're drawing at that location.

6. Drag the mouse to the end point of the new edge you're drawing. When you do, a line stretches from the first anchor point to the current location of the mouse.

> TIP: **Aligning to Axes**
>
> When the line you're drawing is parallel to an axis, the line changes color to match (red=x axis, green=y axis, blue=z axis). In addition, a

ToolTip will appear at the mouse cursor location. Notice also that
when you draw, the line will align to other edges as well for your
convenience. And if you don't want them aligned to other edges,
just keep dragging the mouse until the line snaps to a new alignment.

7. Release the mouse button. When you do, a line appears from the
first anchor point to the current location of the mouse, as shown
in Figure 3.1.

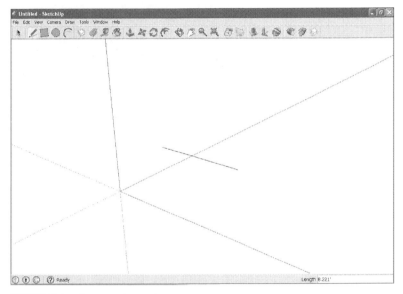

FIGURE 3.1   A new edge.

That's it—you've just drawn an edge.

Drawing Multiline Shapes

You usually don't draw just a single edge when you're using SketchUp;
instead, you draw many connected edges.

It's not hard to draw a new edge connecting to an existing edge in SketchUp. When you're drawing the new edge and approach any existing edges, you'll see a red square appear on the existing edge when you're on that edge. That means that releasing the mouse will connect your new edge to the existing one. When you're near an end point, a circle colored in green will appear on the existing edge at the end point, and a cyan circle will appear for the midpoint,

---

TIP: **Watch the ToolTips**

There's no need to try to memorize the various red squares and cyan or green circles that appear on edges when you're connecting other edges to them—ToolTips will also appear, labeled Endpoint, On Edge, and so on.

So although you can connect one edge to another, it's a little tedious. SketchUp recommends instead that you draw multiple edges all at once, if you can. That way, you can just "connect the dots" to draw a new figure, and SketchUp will keep drawing new edges as long as you move the mouse. Because it realizes you're drawing multiple edges, SketchUp keeps drawing lines until you tell it to stop by hitting the Esc key.

Here's how to use the Line tool to draw multiline figures working with the Engineering–Feet template set in the previous task:

1. Click the **Start Using SketchUp** button and delete the human figure that appears by default.

2. Click the **Line tool** in the toolbar.

3. Move the mouse to the start point of the new edge you're about to draw and click the mouse.

4. Move the mouse to the end point of the new edge—which is also the start point of the new edge—and click it.

5. Repeat step 5 for all the new edges in your drawing. SketchUp will keep drawing edges between the locations you click in your drawing.

6. Press **Esc** to make SketchUp stop drawing edges. SketchUp will stop drawing edges, and your multiline figure is complete, as shown in Figure 3.2.

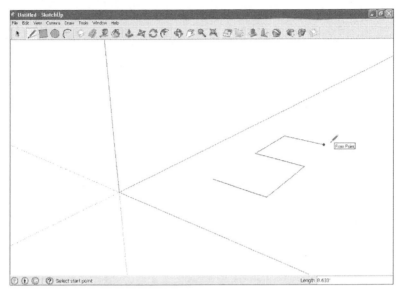

FIGURE 3.2   Drawing a multiline figure.

In this way, SketchUp makes drawing a multi-edge figure easy.

Drawing Measured Lines

You can also tell SketchUp just how long you want your edges to be when you draw them. Note that we are still working with the Engineering–Feet template set in the previous task.

Here's how to draw measured edges:

1. Click the **Start Using SketchUp** button.

2. Click the **Line tool** in the toolbar.

3. Move the mouse to the start point of the new edge you're about to draw and click the mouse.

4. Move the mouse toward the end point of the new edge.

5. Enter the length of the new edge. You can enter the following:

   ▶ **cm** to signify centimeters

   ▶ **m** to signify meters

   ▶ **'** for feet

   ▶ **"** for inches

   Thus, for example, 5m means five meters, 5" means five inches, and so on.

6. Press **Enter.** SketchUp draws the new edge with the length you've requested.

Being able to set the length of edges is crucial for engineering and architectural drawings.

Drawing Rectangles

It takes only two clicks to draw a rectangle in SketchUp. Of course, rectangles are surfaces, so when you're done drawing one, SketchUp will color it as a surface.

Bear in mind that according to SketchUp rules, no rectangle should ever cross another rectangle or any other edge, for that matter. However, it's fine to draw a rectangle so that an edge lies on top of an edge from another figure, such as another rectangle.

Here's how to use the Rectangle tool:

1. Click the **Start Using SketchUp** button and delete the human figure that appears within the Engineering–Feet template.

2. Click the **Rectangle tool** in the toolbar (shown in Figure 3.3).

3. Move the mouse to one corner of the new rectangle you're about to draw and click the mouse.

4. Move the mouse to the opposite corner of the rectangle and click it. SketchUp will draw the rectangle, as shown in Figure 3.3.

As you can see, it's simple to draw rectangles.

The Rectangle
Tool

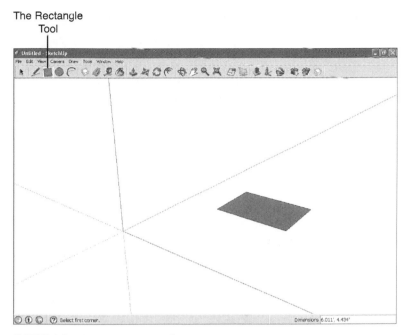

FIGURE 3.3   Drawing a rectangle.

TIP: **Dragging Rectangles**

You can also press the mouse button at one corner of the rectangle and then drag the mouse to the opposite corner, then release the mouse to draw the rectangle. It's easier to click the mouse once in one corner and then in the opposite corner if you're creating measured rectangles. See the next task.

Drawing Measured Rectangles

You can also give SketchUp the dimensions you want your rectangle to be as you draw it.

Here's how to create measured rectangles:

1. Click the **Start Using SketchUp** button and delete the human figure that appears within the Engineering–Feet template.

2. Click the **Rectangle tool** in the toolbar.

3. Move the mouse to one corner of the new rectangle you're about to draw and click the mouse.

4. Move the mouse toward the opposite corner of the new rectangle.

5. Enter the dimensions of the new rectangle, separated by commas. You can enter these units:

   ▶ **cm** to signify centimeters

   ▶ **m** to signify meters

   ▶ **'** for feet

   ▶ **"** for inches.

For example, to draw a rectangle of 5 meters by 6 meters, enter **5m, 6m**.

6. Press **Enter.** SketchUp draws the new rectangle with the length you've requested.

Being able to set the dimensions of rectangles is useful for drawing plans, as in engineering and architectural drawings.

Drawing Circles

The Circle tool does just as you'd expect; it draws circles. That is, it almost does—in fact, what it does is draw 24-sided polygons by default as circles. You can set the number of sides to anything you want, however.

TIP: **The Polygon Tool Versus the Circle Tool**

So circles are really polygons in SketchUp, and they default to 24 sides. Interestingly, SketchUp also has a polygon tool, and it defaults to six sides. But if you set the tools to the same number of sides, they draw identical surfaces. So what's the difference? The difference comes when you push or pull the circle or polygon into 3D, as we'll do soon. No matter how many sides it has, a circle will give you cylindrical sides when you pull it into 3D, whereas a polygon will retain the number of sides the face has on the part that's cylindrical for a circle being dragged into 3D. So if you draw a vertical pillar with a top that's a circle, the sides of the pillar will be a smooth cylinder. But if the top face of the pillar is a polygon, the sides of the pillar will have the same number of sides as the polygon. That's the only real difference between circles and polygons (other than the default number of sides for circles is 24, and the default number of sides for polygons is 6).

Here's how to use the Circle tool:

1. Click the **Start Using SketchUp** button and delete the human figure that appears within the Engineering–Feet template.

2. Click the **Circle tool** in the toolbar (shown in Figure 3.4).

The Circle Tool

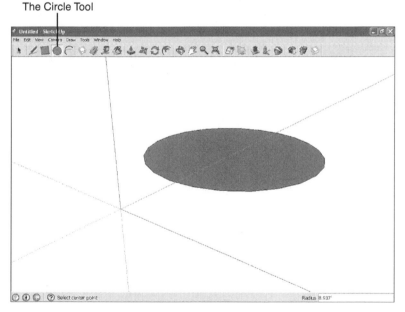

FIGURE 3.4   Drawing a circle.

3. Move the mouse to the location of the center of the circle you want to draw and click the mouse.

4. Move the mouse to the edge of the circle. SketchUp draws the circle as you move the mouse.

5. Click the mouse. SketchUp draws the circle permanently (unless you erase it, of course).

And that's it for drawing circles. When a circle has been drawn, it's a surface, and SketchUp colors it in, as you can see in Figure 3.4.

TIP: **Dragging Circles**

Just as you can with rectangles, you can also press the mouse button at the center of a circle you want to draw, drag the mouse to the edge of the circle, and then release the mouse to draw a circle. It's easier to click the mouse once in the center and then on the edge if you're creating measured circles, however; see the next task.

Drawing Measured Circles

Just as you can with any other figure, you can give SketchUp a size for the circle you're drawing, as you draw it.

Here's how to create measured circles:

1. Click the **Circle tool** in the toolbar.

2. Move the mouse to the location of the center of the circle you want to draw and click the mouse.

3. Move the mouse toward the edge of the new circle.

4. Enter the radius measurement of the new circle. You can enter these units:

▶ **cm** to signify centimeters

▶ **m** to signify meters

▶ **'** for feet

▶ **"** for inches.

For example, to draw a circle with a radius of 5 meters, enter **5m**.

5. Press **Enter**. SketchUp draws the new circle with the radius you've requested.

When the circle has been drawn, it's a surface, as mentioned in the previous task, and SketchUp colors it in.

Drawing Polygons

You can also draw polygons with SketchUp. Presumably because you can draw polygons with the circle tool (see the task after next), the Polygon tool doesn't appear on the Getting Started toolbar that we've been using, so we'll have to use the "large" toolbar here to access the Polygon tool.

Here's how to use the Polygon tool:

1. Click the **Start Using SketchUp** button.

2. Select the **View, Toolbars, Large Tool Set** menu item. This will open the large vertical toolbar you see on the left in Figure 3.5.

The Polygon Tool

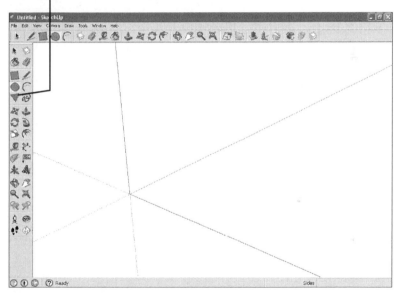

FIGURE 3.5   The large toolset toolbar containing the Polygon tool.

3. Click the **Polygon tool** in the large toolbar (shown in Figure 3.5).

4. Move the mouse to the location of the center of the polygon you want to draw and click the mouse.

5. Move the mouse to the edge of the polygon.

6. Click the mouse. SketchUp draws the polygon.

You can see an example in Figure 3.6.

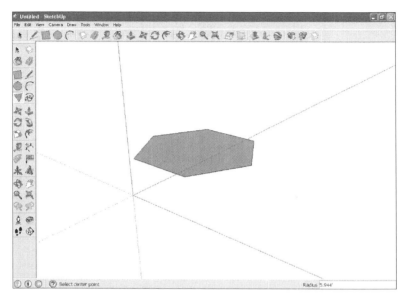

FIGURE 3.6   Drawing a polygon.

NOTE: **Setting the Number of Polygon Sides**

By default, the polygon tool draws six-sided polygons, which might not be what you want—see the task after next to see how to set the number of sides of the polygons you draw.

TIP: **Banishing the Large Toolset Toolbar**

If you want to get rid of the large toolset toolbar when you're done with it, just select the **View, Toolbars, Large Tool Set** menu item again.

Drawing Measured Polygons

Just as you were able with other figures, you can set the size of polygons—which means setting the length of a radius line connecting the center of a polygon to a side so that the connecting line is perpendicular to the side.

Here's how to set the size of polygons:

1. Click the **Start Using SketchUp** button.

2. Select the **View, Toolbars, Large Tool Set** menu item. This will open the large toolset's vertical toolbar.

3. Click the **Polygon tool** in the large toolbar.

4. Move the mouse to the location of the center of the polygon you want to draw and click the mouse.

5. Move the mouse toward the edge of the new polygon.

6. Enter the radius measurement of the new polygon. You can enter these units:

   ▶ **cm** to signify centimeters

   ▶ **m** to signify meters

   ▶ **'** for feet

   ▶ **"** for inches.

   For example, to draw a polygon with a radius of 5 meters, enter **5m**.

7. Press **Enter.** SketchUp draws the new polygon with the radius you've requested.

When the polygon has been drawn, it's a surface, and SketchUp colors it in.

Setting the Number of Sides of Circles or Polygons

By default, the Polygon tool draws polygons of six sides, and the circle tool draws "circles" of 24 sides. But you may need a triangle. So how do you set the number of sides of a figure as you're drawing it?

Follow these steps to set the number of sides of a circle or polygon:

1. If necessary, select the **View, Toolbars, Large Tool Set** menu item.

2. Click the **Polygon** or **Circle tool**. The mouse cursor will change to a pencil with a small six-sided polygon or a circle to indicate you're using the Polygon or Circle tool.

3. Move the mouse to the location of the center of the polygon or circle you want to draw and click the mouse.

4. Move the mouse toward the edge of the polygon or circle. SketchUp draws the polygon or circle as you move the mouse.

5. Type **s** followed by a number to set the number of sides; for example, typing **s3** will create triangles.

6. Move the mouse to the edge of the polygon or circle. SketchUp draws the polygon or circle with the number of sides as you move the mouse.

7. Click the mouse. SketchUp draws the polygon or circle and colors it in as a new surface. You can see an example in Figure 3.7.

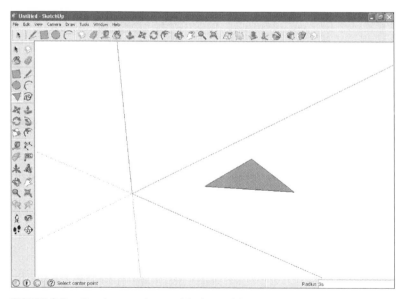

FIGURE 3.7   Drawing a polygon with three sides.

Note that you can use this technique with both the Polygon and Circle tools. The only difference between these two is when you push or pull the figure into 3D (as explained earlier in the "Drawing Circles" task).

Orienting Shapes

By default, when you draw a shape over another shape, the new shape takes the same orientation as the old. So, for example, the circle in Figure 3.8 is drawn by SketchUp to align with the rectangle that's already there.

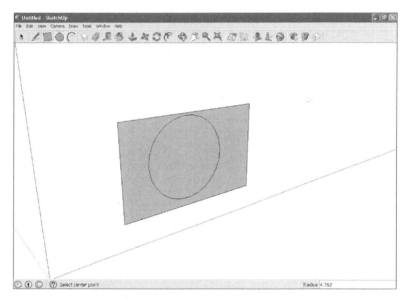

FIGURE 3.8 A circle aligned with a rectangle.

However, you can set the orientation yourself, defeating SketchUp's default orientations. To do that, draw a figure away from any other figure, using the orientation you want, such as creating a horizontal circle. While creating the new figure, press and hold the Shift key. Then draw the figure you want on the surface you want and the figure will retain the orientation of the figure you drew while you started to hold down the Shift key.

In this way, you can orient figures as you want them, despite the orientation of the underlying shape, as shown in Figure 3.9, where we've drawn a horizontal circle over the vertical rectangle (we drew the horizontal circle at right to show SketchUp the orientation we want, and held the Shift key down as we drew that first horizontal circle to hold the orientation for the second horizontal circle, drawn over the vertical rectangle).

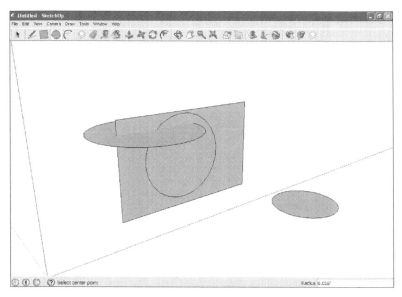

FIGURE 3.9   A new circle with a custom alignment.

Getting Information About Shapes

You can get information about shapes in SketchUp, such as the shape's area and number of sides. Just follow these steps:

1. Click the **Start Using SketchUp** button. Click the human figure that appears in the Engineering–Feet template by default to select it and press the **Delete** key to delete it.

2. Draw a shape.

3. Right-click the shape and select the **Entity Information** menu item. When you do, you get an information box showing information about the shape, as shown in Figure 3.10.

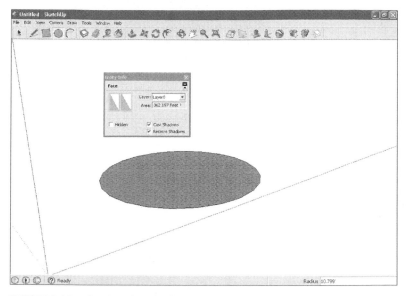

FIGURE 3.10   Getting shape information.

4. To get information about the edge of the shape, click the **Select tool** in the toolbar while the Information dialog box is open, then click the edge of the shape. When you do, the information box changes, showing information about the shape's edge, as shown in Figure 3.11.

TIP: **Changing a Shape's Size or Number of Edges**

You can edit the information in a shape's Information box, changing the shape itself. For example, you can change the number of edges a polygon has by entering a new number in the Segments box and pressing **Enter**.

The Select Tool

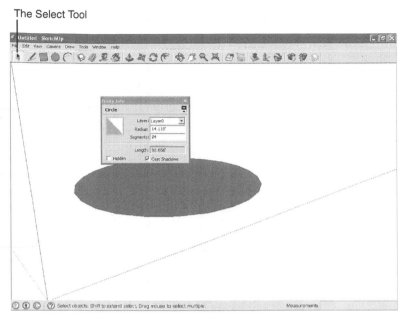

FIGURE 3.11   Getting information about the edge of a shape.

Saving Your Work

Now that you've been creating shapes, it's time to see how to save your work:

1. Select the File menu's **Save As** menu item. SketchUp opens a Save As dialog box. Enter the name of the file you want to save your work in the Filename box. Note that SketchUp files use the .skp extension.

2. Navigate to the directory where you want to save your file. Use the standard clickable folders that appear in the dialog box.

3. Click the **Save** button in the dialog box. Your file is saved and the dialog box disappears.

When you're working and want to save your work at some point after having created a file following the previous steps, select the File menu's **Save** menu item.

Drawing Shapes: Arcs, Freehand, Text, and 3D Text

In this lesson, we cover how to draw arcs, how to draw freehand, and how to draw text.

Arcs, Freehand, and Text

There's a lot to see here—particularly with arcs, because they're a common edge element you use to draw curves in models. Drawing freehand is also cool, but a little hard to control because you draw with the mouse. Finally, we'll see how to draw text in both 2D and 3D.

Let's get started with arcs.

Drawing Arcs

Drawing arcs is a three-step process in SketchUp—you click at one anchor point, click at another, and then pull the arc (SketchUp will bend it as you pull) into place.

> TIP: **An Arc Actually Has 12 Sides**
> Just as circles are made up, by default, of 24 sides in SketchUp (see Lesson 2, "Up and Running with SketchUp"), arcs are made up of 12 segments. If you're drawing a large arc, those sides, which are really line segments, might be visible. To fix that, you can set the number of sides in an arc. We'll see how in the task "Setting the Number of Arc Segments," a bit later.

Let's take a look at how to create arcs now.

1. Click the **Start Using SketchUp** button and click the human figure that appears in the Engineering–Feet template to select it; press the Del key to delete it.

2. Click the **Arc tool** in the toolbar (shown in Figure 4.1).

The Arc Tool

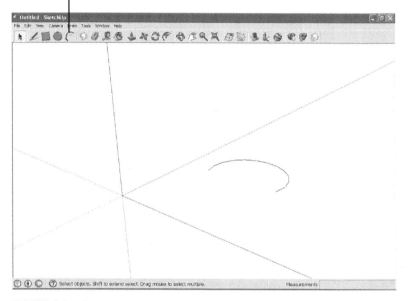

FIGURE 4.1   The Arc tool and a new arc.

3. Move the mouse to the start point of the new arc you're about to draw and click the mouse. When you do, you anchor an end point of the arc you're drawing at that location.

4. Move the mouse to the end point of the new arc you're drawing and click the mouse. When you do, a line appears from the first anchor point to the current location of the mouse.

5. Slide the mouse along the line between the two end points, and move the mouse to "pull" the line out into an arc. When you do, an arc appears from the first anchor point to the current location of the mouse.

> TIP: **Inferring Arcs to Planes**
>
> Note that as you stretch your arc, SketchUp will infer it to different axes or underlying surfaces (that is, draw it in the plane defined by two axes or an underlying surface). Keep pulling the arc until it snaps to the plane you want to draw it in, if that becomes an issue.

6. Click the mouse. The arc becomes permanent (unless you erase it, of course). You can see an arc in Figure 4.1.

That's it—you've just drawn an arc.

> TIP: **Drawing Perfect Half Circles**
>
> Want to draw a perfect half circle? Just keep pulling an arc until the ToolTip at the location of the mouse reads Half Circle; then click the mouse.

Drawing Measured Arcs

Perhaps you want to create an arc a bit more precisely than you can freehand. You can specify the radius of any arc; here's how:

1. Click the **Start Using SketchUp** button and click the human figure that appears in the Engineering–Feet template to select it; press the Del key to delete it.

2. Click the **Arc tool** in the toolbar (shown in Figure 4.1).

3. Move the mouse to the start point of the new arc you're about to draw and click the mouse. When you do, you anchor an end point of the arc you're drawing at that location.

4. Move the mouse to the end point of the new arc you're drawing and click the mouse. When you do, a line appears from the first anchor point to the current location of the mouse.

5. Slide the mouse along the line between the two end points, and move the mouse to "pull" the line out into an arc. When you do, an arc appears from the first anchor point to the current location of the mouse.

6. Enter the size of the radius you want (simply stop using the mouse and type in the radius; no dialog box or text field appears). You can use the following:

   ▶ **cm** to signify centimeters

   ▶ **m** to signify meters

   ▶ **'** for feet

   ▶ **"** for inches.

   Thus, for example, 5m means five meters, 5" means five inches, and so on.

7. Press **Enter.** SketchUp draws the new arc with the radius you've requested.

And there you have it—an arc with a specific radius.

Drawing Arcs Tangent to Corners

Consider the shape in Figure 4.2. Suppose that you want to round the acute angle in that figure—how would you do it?

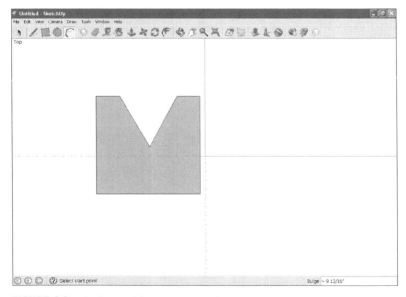

FIGURE 4.2   A shape with an acute angle.

You could draw an arc so that it was tangent to the two sides, as shown in Figure 4.3.

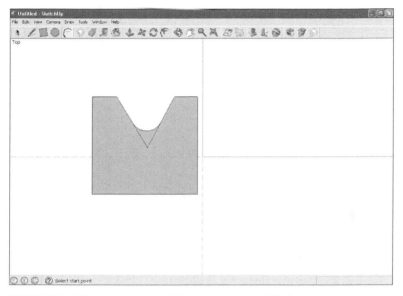

FIGURE 4.3   The same shape with a tangent arc added.

Then you could use the Eraser tool to erase the unneeded acute angle, as shown in Figure 4.4.

That's it—you've rounded the acute angle. Here's how it works step by step:

1. Click the **Start Using SketchUp** button and delete the human figure that appears in Engineering–Feet.

2. Draw the surface similar to the one shown in Figure 4.2 with the angle you want to round.

3. Click the **Arc tool** in the toolbar and move the mouse to the start point of the new arc you're about to draw. The start point should be on an edge adjacent to the angle you want to round.

4. Click the mouse. When you do, you anchor an end point of the arc you're drawing at that location.

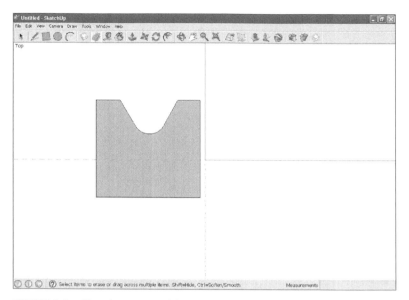

FIGURE 4.4   The shape now with a rounded arc.

5. Move the mouse to the end point of the new arc you're drawing and click the mouse. When you do, a line appears from the first anchor point to the current location of the mouse.

6. Slide the mouse along the line between the two end points, and move the mouse to "pull" the line out into an arc. When you've pulled the arc such so its sides are exactly tangent to the sides adjacent to the angle you're rounding, the arc will turn cyan. That's your clue that you've selected the correct arc.

7. Click the mouse. The arc becomes permanent (unless you erase it, of course).

8. Click the **Eraser tool** in the toolbar. The Eraser tool looks just like, well, an eraser and is a couple tools to the right of the Arc tool. The mouse cursor changes to a small eraser to indicate you're using the Eraser tool.

9. Click the two line segments inside the shape that formed the acute angle to erase them. This gives you Figure 4.4.

Rounding acute corners like this is a useful skill when you're using SketchUp.

Drawing Multiple Tangent Arcs

What if you wanted to draw a series of multiple arcs, such as those that appear in Figure 4.5?

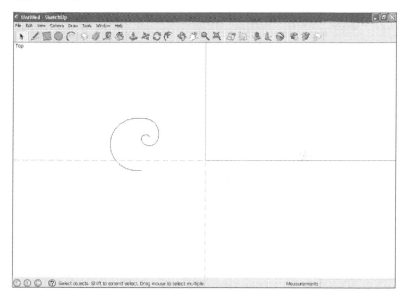

FIGURE 4.5   Multiple connected arcs.

The trick is making each new arc tangent to the previous arc so that the series of arcs appears smooth—and SketchUp can help. Here's how:

1. Click the **Start Using SketchUp** button and delete the human figure that appears in the Engineering–Feet template by default.

2. Click the **Arc tool** in the toolbar and move the mouse to the start point of the new arc you're about to draw.

3. Move the mouse to the start point of the new arc you're about to draw and click the mouse. When you do, you anchor an end point of the arc you're drawing at the location.

4. Move the mouse to the end point of the new arc you're drawing and click the mouse. When you do, a line appears from the first anchor point to the current location of the mouse.

5. Slide the mouse along the line between the two end points, and move the mouse to "pull" the line out into an arc and click the mouse. The arc becomes permanent (unless you erase it, of course).

6. Click the end point of the arc you want to continue and move the mouse away from the end point. As you do, SketchUp will draw a new arc in blue tangent to the old arc.

7. Move the mouse to the new arc's end point and click the mouse. The new arc becomes permanent.

8. Repeat steps 6 and 7 for additional arcs.

That's it—now you can draw all kinds of fancy spirals.

Setting the Number of Arc Segments

By default, arcs have twelve sides, but you can change that to any number of sides you want. Here's how:

1. Click the **Start Using SketchUp** button and click the human figure that appears in the Engineering–Feet template to select it; press the Del key to delete it.

2. Click the **Arc tool** in the toolbar (shown previously in Figure 4.1).

3. Move the mouse to the start point of the new arc you're about to draw and click the mouse. When you do, you anchor an end point of the arc you're drawing at that location.

4. Move the mouse to the end point of the new arc you're drawing and click the mouse. When you do, a line appears from the first anchor point to the current location of the mouse.

5. Slide the mouse along the line between the two end points, and move the mouse to "pull" the line out into an arc. When you do, an arc appears from the first anchor point to the current location of the mouse.

6. Type the number of sides you want, followed by "s." For example, **5s** will give you a five-sided arc.

7. Press **Enter**. The arc changes to have the number of sides you've requested.

8. Continue pulling the arc into position.

9. Click the mouse. The arc becomes permanent. Figure 4.6 shows a five-sided arc.

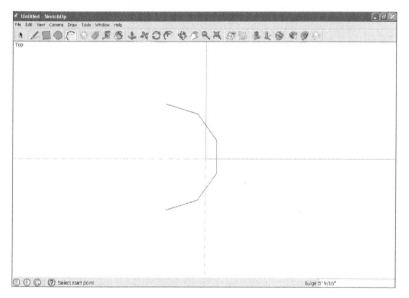

FIGURE 4.6   A five-sided arc.

And now you can draw arcs with as many sides as you want.

Drawing Freehand

Drawing freehand couldn't be easier in one sense—you just drag the mouse; but it also couldn't be harder in another—if you want to draw figures with any accuracy, it's extraordinarily difficult to do so with the mouse.

NOTE: **You're Not Actually Drawing Freehand**

If you were actually drawing entirely freehand, each location of the mouse would appear as a dot as you moved over it. But because there are only a limited number of mouse events per second, SketchUp draws the mouse locations it gets and then connects the dots with line segments. So if you draw very rapidly, your figures might end up looking more like interconnected lines.

Here's how to use the freehand tool:

1. Click the **Start Using SketchUp** button and click the human figure that appears in the Engineering–Feet template to select it; press the Del key to delete it.

2. Select the **View, Toolbars, Large Tool Set** menu item. This will open the large toolset toolbar.

3. Click the **Freehand tool** in the large toolbar (as shown in Figure 4.7).

4. Move the mouse to the location you want to start drawing from.

5. Press the mouse button and drag the mouse to draw the figure you want. SketchUp draws the figure following the mouse.

You can see an example in Figure 4.7.

Note that you can't "fix" a freehand drawing on the pixel level in SketchUp—the only practical thing is to start over.

The Freehand Tool

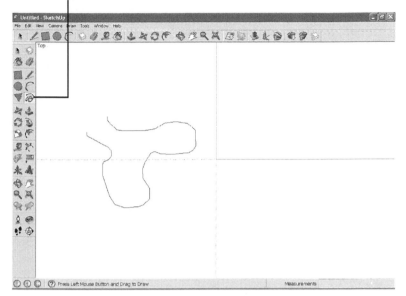

FIGURE 4.7   Drawing freehand with the Freehand tool.

Drawing Surfaces Freehand

In addition to freehand figures of the kind you see in Figure 4.7, you can also draw complete surfaces in SketchUp. After you complete a surface, SketchUp will color it in automatically.

Essentially, you draw freehand figures as detailed in the previous task with an additional step: Close the figure you're drawing. When you close the figure, SketchUp can treat it as a completed surface and fills it in. You can see a few surfaces drawn freehand in Figure 4.8.

Note that it's quite difficult to draw accurate surfaces freehand, and that you usually draw elaborate surfaces as conglomerations of simpler surfaces from the toolbar.

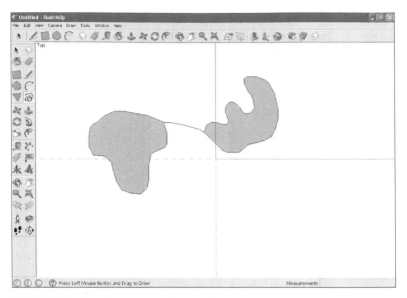

FIGURE 4.8   Drawing surfaces freehand.

Drawing Text

You can also draw text in SketchUp, and sometimes that's crucial, as when you might want to label the parts of an architectural drawing. For example, take a look at Figure 4.9, which shows a cube, and some text, "Cube."

How did that text get there? Here's how:

1. Click the **Start Using SketchUp** button and click the human figure that appears in the Engineering–Feet template to select it; press the Del key to delete it.

2. Select the **View**, **Toolbars**, **Large Tool Set** menu item. This will open the large toolset toolbar.

3. Click the **Text tool** in the large toolbar. The Text tool is the one that displays the letters ABC (as shown in Figure 4.9).

The Text Tool

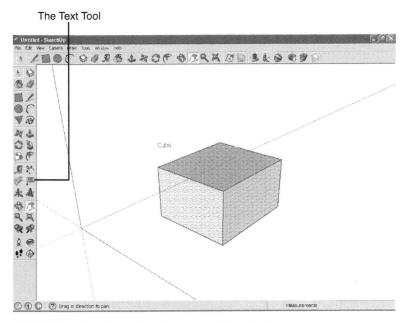

FIGURE 4.9 The Text tool and some text in a drawing.

4. Move the mouse to the location you want to place your text and click the mouse. A box with the prompt Enter Text appears at the location of the mouse for you to enter text in.

5. Enter your text.

6. Click outside the box to make the box's outline disappear.

It's important to realize that this text is free-floating; it's not part of the model you're drawing. Thus, for example, if you use the Pan tool to move the cube, the text doesn't follow, as you see in Figure 4.10.

So how do you connect text to a model or surface so that it will move and orbit with that model or surface? Take a look at the next task.

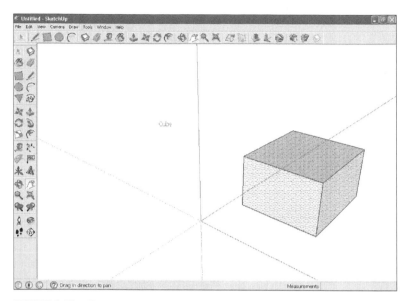

FIGURE 4.10   Text stays in place as you move the model.

TIP: **The Proper Use for Screen Text**

A good use for the free-floating screen text displayed by the steps in this task is to label an entire drawing. Then the drawing label doesn't change, no matter how you change the model view.

Annotating Objects with Text

Sometimes, you might want to annotate objects you're drawing with text, as shown in Figure 4.11, where we've drawn a cube and labeled it.

In contrast to the previous task, where we just added text to the drawing, this time we've annotated an object in the drawing—the cube. Now when you pan and orbit, the annotation text follows the object, as you can see in Figure 4.12.

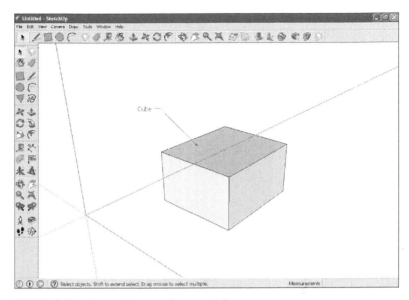

FIGURE 4.11 Annotation text for a model.

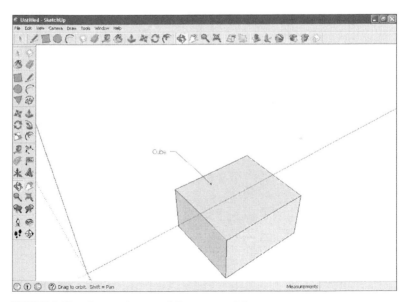

FIGURE 4.12 Annotation text follows a model.

So how do you annotate an object and connect text with an arrow pointing to an object? Just follow these steps:

1. Click the **Start Using SketchUp** button and click the human figure that appears in the Engineering–Feet template to select it; press the Del key to delete it.

2. Select the **View**, **Toolbars**, **Large Tool Set** menu item. This will open the large toolset toolbar.

3. Click the **Text tool** in the large toolbar (as shown previously in Figure 4.9).

4. Press the mouse button on the surface or edge you want to annotate.

5. Drag the mouse to the location where you want the text to appear and release the mouse button. A text box appears at the location at which you released the mouse button.

   By default, the area of a surface will appear as the text in the text box if you're annotating a surface, and the length of an edge if you're annotating an edge.

6. Enter your text.

7. Click outside the box to make the box's outline disappear.

Now you're able to annotate objects in your drawings.

Setting Text Properties

What if you wanted to display your annotation text in a large, italic font, as shown in Figure 4.13?

Just follow these steps to customize your text:

1. Click the **Select tool**. The mouse cursor will change to an arrow.

2. Right-click the text whose properties you want to change. A context menu appears.

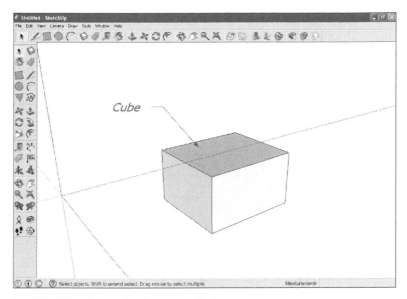

FIGURE 4.13   Annotating in large italic text.

3. Select the **Entity Info** menu item. SketchUp displays a dialog
   box labeled Entity Info.

4. Click the **Change Font** button in the Entity Info dialog box. The
   Font dialog box appears, as shown in Figure 4.14.

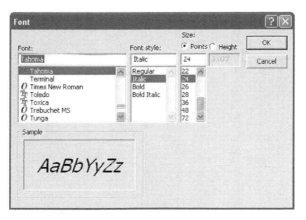

FIGURE 4.14   Setting text properties.

5. Select the **Font**, **Font Style**, and **Size** you want for the text in the Font dialog box.

6. Click the **OK** button to close the Font dialog box.

7. Click the **X** button at the upper right to close the Entity Info dialog box. SketchUp adjusts the text as you've requested.

These steps let you change the font of one selection of text. But what if you have a dozen text items all around the screen?

You can change all the text in your drawing at once if you select **Model Info** from the **Window** menu. The dialog box you see in Figure 4.15 appears.

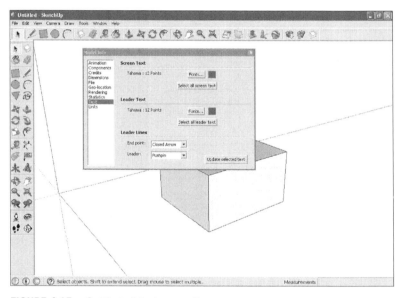

FIGURE 4.15   Setting all text properties.

Select the Text item in the left pane. To set the properties of free-floating screen text, click the **Select All Screen Text** button, and then click the **Font** button above it to display the Font dialog box, which will let you set the text properties for all screen text.

To set the text properties of the text used for annotation, click the **Select All Leader Text** button and then click the **Font** button above it to display the Font dialog box. You can then set the text properties for all annotation text.

> TIP: **Setting Arrows for Text**
>
> In the Entity Info box, you can also change the text displayed, as well as the style of arrow used to connect the text to the surface or edge.

Drawing 3D Text

SketchUp also lets you draw 3D text with the 3D text tool. For example, take a look at the 3D text that appears in Figure 4.16.

The 3D Text Tool

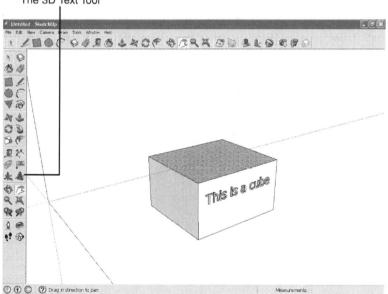

FIGURE 4.16 Using the 3D text tool.

It's important to note that 3D text is treated as a shape, unlike 2D text. 3D text becomes part of the model, whereas standard 2D screen text does not. And even while annotated text becomes part of the model, it's only there to tag parts of the model, not become part of it. The text in Figure 4.16 is part of the model and appears as a structural element in the model.

So, whereas 2D text is used for labeling, 3D text becomes a structural element in the model itself.

> TIP: **Making 2D Text Part of the Model**
>
> Want to make 2D text part of the model? Just use 3D text, setting the text "extrusion" (see step 6) to zero.

Here's how to draw in 3D:

1. Click the **Start Using SketchUp** button and click the human figure that appears in the Engineering–Feet template to select it; press the Del key to delete it.

2. Select the **View**, **Toolbars**, **Large Tool Set** menu item. This opens the large toolset toolbar.

3. Click the **3D Text tool** in the large toolbar (shown in Figure 4.16). The dialog box, labeled Place 3D Text, appears, as you see in Figure 4.17.

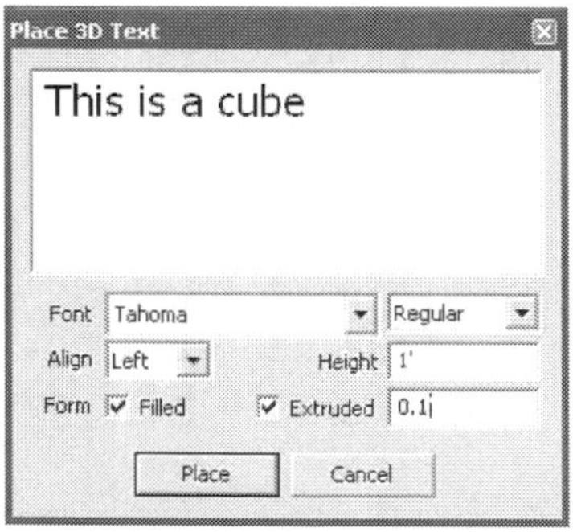

FIGURE 4.17   Customizing 3D text.

4. Enter the text you want to make 3D in the large text box.

5. Select the **Font, Alignment, Text style (Regular or Bold)**, and whether you want the characters to appear filled in.

6. Enter the height of the characters you want (using ' for feet, " for inches, m for meters, or cm for centimeters) in the Height box and the 3D depth you want to give to the characters in the Extruded box.

7. Click the **Place** button. The dialog box disappears, and the text appears as a model element that is selected and that moves as the mouse moves.

8. Move the mouse to move the text and then click the mouse to place the text in the model. The text will align to any axis or surface, just as any other model element.

That's it—you can now add 3D text to models using the 3D Text tool.

LESSON 5

Going 3D

In this lesson, we're going to see what SketchUp is really all about—going 3D.

Getting Started

SketchUp's 3D capabilities are what set it apart from the rest of the pack of drawing tools. You're going to see how easy it is to create 3D models in SketchUp. Although you might think that you need to draw every edge to make a model 3D, that's not true—SketchUp operates in a very clever way to give you 3D power.

All you need to do is to draw a 2D surface (and remember, such surfaces can be aligned to any plane). Then you use one of SketchUp's 3D tools, such as the Push/Pull tool, to pull it into 3D. Thus a rectangle becomes a cube, for example.

The Push/Pull tool, which works on any surface that's in one plane, is the primary 3D tool in SketchUp. This tool lets you push or pull surfaces into 3D in a way that's quite impressive. But other tools in SketchUp have 3D power as well, such as the Move tool, which we'll also see here.

You can use the Move tool to move objects around, of course. But when you first use the Select tool to select an edge, you can use the Move tool to pull out that edge in such a way that the connected surface follows, while still being anchored on the opposite edge (think of opening a cabinet door).

We'll see both the Push/Pull and Move tools in this lesson, along with some auxiliary tools, the Select tool and the Eraser tool.

This is a big lesson for us, because it's all about 3D, and that's also what SketchUp is all about—3D.

Let's get started immediately with the Push/Pull tool.

Pulling Objects into 3D

You need to start with a basic shape or surface. For this task we'll keep things simple and use a rectangle. (Refer to Lesson 3, "Drawing Shapes: Lines, Rectangles, Polygons, and Circles" for more.)

Use the Rectangle tool to create a rectangle similar to what you see in Figure 5.1.

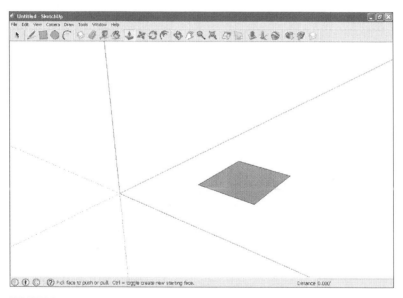

FIGURE 5.1   A rectangle.

Now, what you really want is a cube, so to transform the rectangle, we'll use the Push/Pull tool, as shown in Figure 5.2.

The Push/Pull Tool

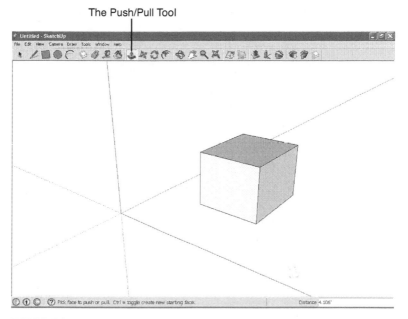

FIGURE 5.2   The Push/Pull tool and the resulting cube.

When you use the Push/Pull tool (shown in Figure 5.2), you literally pull the rectangle into a 3D shape. This tool is at the center of what SketchUp does for you, so it's an important one to learn.

Here's how to go 3D with SketchUp and the Push/Pull tool:

1. Click the **Start Using SketchUp** button and click the human figure that appears in the Engineering–Feet template to select it; press the Del key to delete it.

2. Draw a shape.

3. Click the **Push/Pull tool** in the toolbar (shown in Figure 5.2).

4. Move the mouse cursor to the surface you want to pull or push into 3D. Note that the surface must be flat.

5. Press the mouse button on the surface and drag the surface in the direction you want to extend it into 3D.

> TIP: **Pushing or Pulling Surfaces**
>
> Note that you can only push or pull surfaces perpendicular to themselves.

As you drag the mouse, the surface pulls into 3D. The sides of the new 3D shape are defined by the edges of the 2D shape.

6. Release the mouse button. The object becomes 3D, as you can see in Figure 5.2. As you can see, pulling shapes into 3D is one the coolest features in SketchUp.

Pushing Objects into 3D

In the previous task, you saw that you could pull a free-standing rectangle into 3D. But now take a look at Figure 5.3.

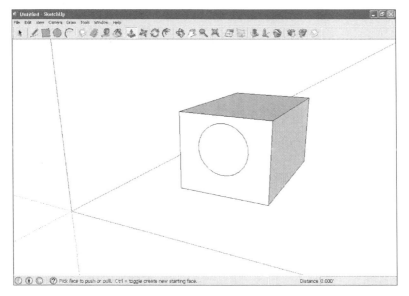

FIGURE 5.3   A cube with an attached circle.

Can you pull the attached circle into a cylinder? Yes, you can. In fact, now you have two options. Because the circle is attached to an existing 3D surface, you have the option of not only pulling the circle out of the cube, but you can also *push* the cylinder into the cube.

Here's how:

1. Click the **Start Using SketchUp** button and click the human figure that appears in the Engineering–Feet template to select it; press the Del key to delete it.

2. Draw the cube as shown in Figure 5.3.

3. Draw a circle on the cube using the Circle tool, as shown in Figure 5.3.

4. Click the **Push/Pull tool** in the toolbar.

5. Move the mouse cursor to the circle and press the mouse button on the circle.

6. Drag the circle out of the cube to pull it into 3D, or push it into the cube to push it into 3D. You can see the circle pulled into 3D in Figure 5.4 and pushed into the cube in Figure 5.5.

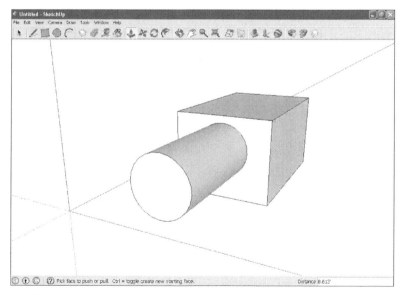

FIGURE 5.4   Pulling a circle into a cylinder.

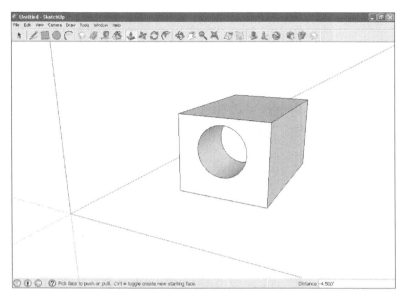

FIGURE 5.5　Pushing a cylinder into a cube.

7. Release the mouse button. The cylinder becomes 3D.

Now you can both pull and push objects into 3D.

Using Measured Push/Pull

What if you wanted to push or pull an object exactly 5 feet when making it 3D? That is, suppose you have a circle on one surface of a cube (refer to Figure 5.3), and you want to pull the circle out into a cylinder exactly 5 feet—could you do it?

Yes. Like most SketchUp operations, you can interrupt them midway and enter a measurement. Here's how it works when you're pushing or pulling objects into 3D—in this example, we'll pull a cylinder out of a cube by 5 feet:

1. Click the **Start Using SketchUp** button and click the human figure that appears in the Engineering–Feet template to select it; press the Del key to delete it.

2. Draw the cube with a circle on one surface.

3. Click the **Push/Pull tool** in the toolbar.

4. Move the mouse cursor to the circle and press the mouse button on the circle.

5. Drag the circle out of the cube to pull it into 3D, or push it into the cube to push it into 3D.

6. Release the mouse button. The cylinder becomes 3D.

7. Enter the length of the 3D object you want. In this example, we'll create a 5-foot cylinder. Enter a length and then the units— you can use these units:

   ▶ **cm** to signify centimeters

   ▶ **m** to signify meters

   ▶ ' for feet

   ▶ " for inches

   Thus, 5m means five meters, 5" means five inches, and so on. In this example, we'll use 5 feet, 5', giving you the cylinder you see in Figure 5.6.

8. Press **Enter.** SketchUp changes the new 3D object's length to match what you've requested.

Note that when you release the mouse button the first time, it feels as though you've finished drawing the cylinder, but SketchUp remembers that the cylinder is still being drawn, and if you enter a length and press Enter, it'll apply that length to the most recent figure, which in this example is the cylinder.

Inferring Push/Pull

Suppose you wanted to draw two cubes to the same height, similar to what you can see in Figure 5.7, but are not satisfied with your first effort.

Can SketchUp help make the two cubes the same height?

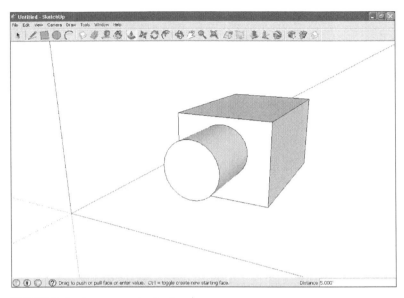

FIGURE 5.6　A measured cylinder.

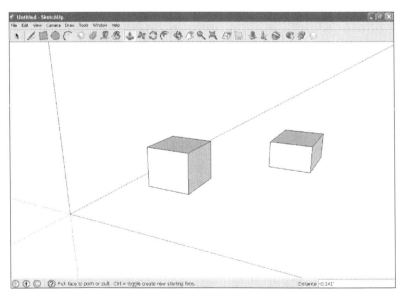

FIGURE 5.7　Two cubes.

Yes, it can—through inferring. Because it's so common when creating models to want one object to match another in some dimension (think of the length of table legs, for example), SketchUp allows you to set an object's length by referring to another object that already has the length you want. This process is called inferring (See Lesson 2, "Up and Running with SketchUp").

When drawing 3D objects, you can infer the length on one object to another object, making the first object's length match the second object. Here's how it works in the example of the two cubes in Figure 5.7:

1. Click the **Start Using SketchUp** button and click the human figure that appears in the Engineering–Feet template to select it; press the Del key to delete it.

2. Draw two rectangles in the x-y plane.

3. Click the **Push/Pull tool** in the toolbar.

4. Pull the rectangles into cubes of different heights, as shown in Figure 5.7.

5. With the Push/Pull tool, click the top surface of one of the cubes.

6. Move the mouse to the top surface of the other cube. A dotted blue line extends from the first surface to the surface you're inferring, as shown in Figure 5.8, and the first cube (the one you clicked first) snaps to the height of the second cube (the one you're inferring to), as you can see in the figure.

7. Click the top surface of the second cube. The height of the first cube becomes frozen to match the height of the second cube.

Inferring provides an easy way to make the length of objects match in SketchUp.

Cutting Openings

Another cool feature that you will want to take advantage of in SketchUp is using the Push/Pull tool to "cut" or create the illusion of openings in shapes.

Suppose you've just drawn a rectangle that represents a wall. For example, see the wall in Figure 5.9.

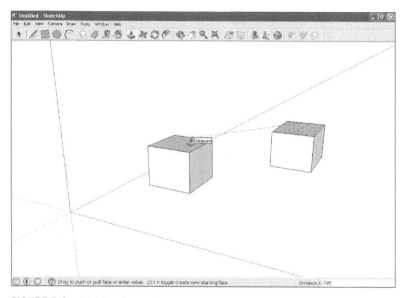

FIGURE 5.8   Making the cubes equal height.

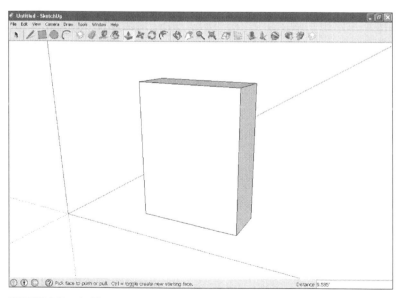

FIGURE 5.9   A 3D wall.

Now say that you want to cut a window into that wall. How could you do it?

The Push/Pull tool has a special property—you can cut objects right out of existing 3D objects. Here's how it works:

1. Click the **Start Using SketchUp** button and click the human figure that appears in the Engineering–Feet template to select it; press the Del key to delete it.

2. Draw the 3D wall, such as the one you see in Figure 5.9.

3. Draw the 2D outline of the window you want to cut into the wall. You might use a rectangle, as shown in Figure 5.10.

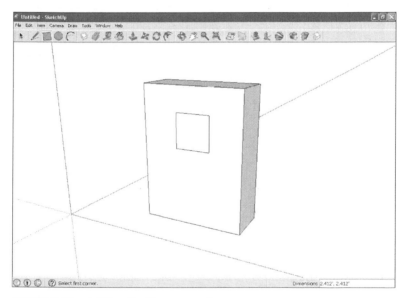

FIGURE 5.10   A 3D wall with a rectangle.

4. Click the **Push/Pull tool** in the toolbar.

5. Push the window outline through the wall to the other side. The part you've pushed disappears, leaving a cutout, as you can see in Figure 5.11.

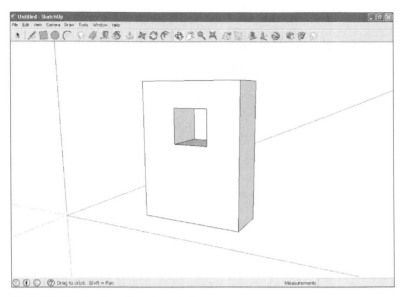

FIGURE 5.11   A 3D wall with a window.

So that's the trick—to create a cutout, push a shape through a 3D object until the shape disappears. Very cool.

Erasing Edges with the Eraser Tool

You can use the Eraser tool to erase edges, and that can help when you're going 3D. For example, take a look at the block in Figure 5.12.

Suppose you wanted to push the rectangle you see on the block through to create an opening, but SketchUp won't let you cut out the opening. What's wrong? And, how can you fix it?

For this task we will use the Orbit tool (refer to Lesson 2) and the Eraser tool (introduced in Lesson 4, "Drawing Shapes: Arcs, Freehand, Text, and 3D Text"). Follow these steps to solve the most common problem when cutting openings:

1. Click the **Orbit tool** in the toolbar.

2. Orbit around the entire 3D object you're trying to push an opening through.

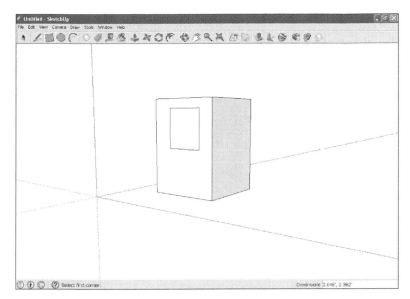

FIGURE 5.12   A 3D block with rectangle.

3. Search for obstructing edges—SketchUp won't push openings
through edges. In the case of the object in Figure 5.12, it turns
out that there's an edge drawn across the back of the object, as
you can see in Figure 5.13. This edge will stop SketchUp from
pushing an opening through the object.

4. To get rid of unwanted edges, select the **Eraser tool** in the toolbar.

TIP: **The Eraser Tool Is Only to Erase Edges**

In SketchUp, you use the Eraser tool only to erase edges. But if
you want to get rid of a surface, it's easy—just erase all its edges.

---

5. Click the unwanted edge. When you do, that edge disappears.

6. Push the rectangle through the object to the other side with the
Push/Pull tool. The part you've pushed disappears, leaving a
cutout, as you can see in Figure 5.14.

So that's the way you use the Eraser tool—to erase unwanted edges. And
if you want to get rid of a surface, erase its edges.

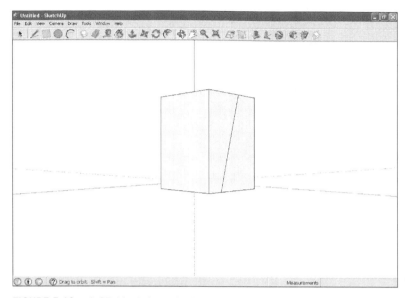

FIGURE 5.13   A 3D block from the back, showing a blocking edge.

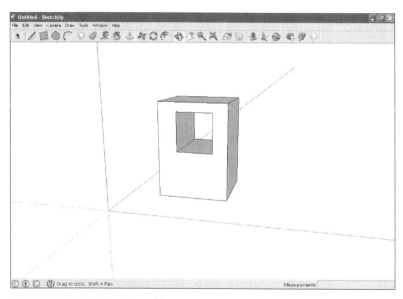

FIGURE 5.14   A 3D object with a cutout.

Selecting Edges and Surfaces with the Select Tool

Now that you've mastered drawing surfaces and are working with 3D objects, it's time to see how to select edges, surfaces, and objects using the Select tool.

Knowing how to select edges, surfaces, and objects is important for many actions in SketchUp, because you often have to indicate to SketchUp just what item you're working with. For example, when you want to make a copy of an object, you start by selecting that object. Selecting an object brings it to SketchUp's attention by telling it just what item you're working with. When you want to use the Move tool to pull out an edge from an object into 3D, you start by selecting that edge.

When you select an object, SketchUp indicates your selection by drawing it in a slightly different color than it was before, or by making it appear dotted. After you've selected an item, you can use that item as the target of your following operations, as we'll see. For example, if you had three boxes and wanted to make copies of only one, you'd start by selecting the box you want to make copies of, and then the appropriate menu choices to copy the item, as we're going to see in this lesson.

Selecting surfaces and edges is easy. Just click the **Select tool** in the Getting Started toolbar (recall the Select tool has an arrow as its icon, and is the first tool on the left in the Getting Started toolbar), and click the surface or edge you want to select.

When you select a surface, SketchUp fills the surface with blue dots. When you select an edge, SketchUp colors it blue.

Selecting an entire object is also easy, because the Select tool lets you draw selection rectangles automatically. Just press the mouse button outside the object and drag the mouse over the object to draw a selection rectangle, as you see in Figure 5.15.

When you release the mouse button, the entire object will be selected (and you can use menu selections to copy it, move it, and so on), which means all its surfaces will be dotted in blue, and its edges will be drawn in blue.

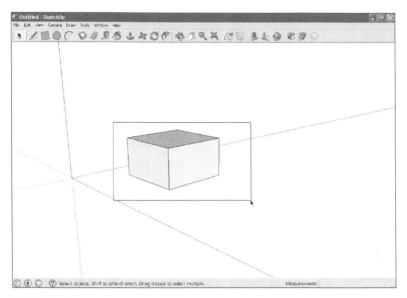

FIGURE 5.15   Drawing a selection rectangle.

Now we know how to select edges, surfaces, and objects. Let's start putting that knowledge to work in the next task.

Copying Objects

You'll often want to copy elements in SketchUp. For example, we're going to construct a table later on in this lesson by creating one table leg and then making a few copies for the other legs. Copying objects guarantees you exact duplicates when having an exact duplicate is important—as when you're making actual table legs.

Being able to copy objects is an essential skill in SketchUp, so here's how you do it. In this case, we'll make a copy of a simple cube:

1. Click the **Start Using SketchUp** button and click the human figure that appears in the Engineering–Feet template to select it; press the Del key to delete it.

2. Draw a horizontal rectangle.

3. Click the **Push/Pull tool** in the toolbar.

4. Move the mouse cursor to the rectangle and press the mouse button on the rectangle.

5. Press the mouse button on the rectangle and drag the rectangle up to extend it into a 3D cube, as shown in Figure 5.16.

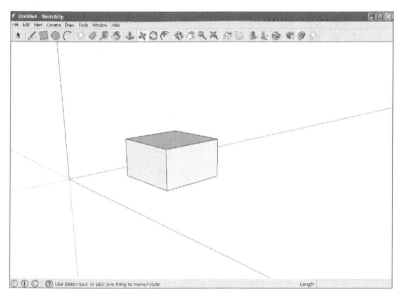

FIGURE 5.16   Drawing a cube.

6. Click the **Select tool** in the toolbar.

7. Select the cube by pressing the mouse button outside it and dragging the selection rectangle that appears over the cube. Now you've selected the object you want to copy.

8. Select the Edit menu's **Copy** item.

9. Select the Edit menu's **Paste** item. When you do, a copy of the object appears at the location of the mouse cursor. Moving the mouse cursor moves the copy of the object.

10. Move the mouse cursor to the location at which you want to place the copy of the object.

11. Click the mouse. The copy of the object appears at the location you clicked the mouse and stops moving around with the mouse cursor. You can see an example in Figure 5.17, where we've copied the cube.

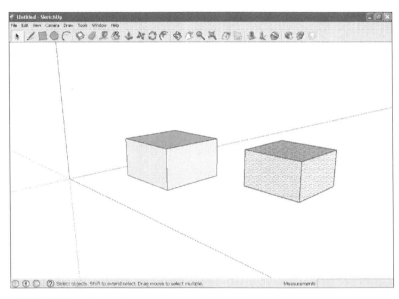

FIGURE 5.17   Copying a cube.

That's it—now you can copy objects.

Moving Edges and Surfaces with the Move Tool

You can use the Move tool to pull edges into 3D. Take a look at the cube in Figure 5.18.

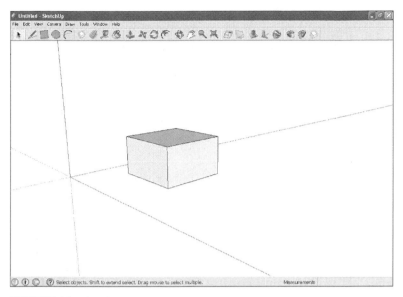

FIGURE 5.18   A cube.

That's fine—but what if you wanted to draw a ramp instead, such as the one you see in Figure 5.19?

You can easily convert the cube in Figure 5.18 to the ramp in Figure 5.19 using the Move tool, which you can use to grasp edges and pull them into 3D (the Push/Pull tool lets you only push or pull surfaces).

Here's how it works—in this example, we'll convert a cube to a ramp.

1. Click the **Start Using SketchUp** button and click the human figure that appears in the Engineering–Feet template to select it; press the Del key to delete it.

2. Draw a horizontal rectangle.

3. Click the **Push/Pull tool** in the toolbar and move the mouse cursor to the rectangle.

4. Press the mouse button on the rectangle and drag the rectangle up to extend it into a 3D cube, as shown in Figure 5.18.

The Move Tool

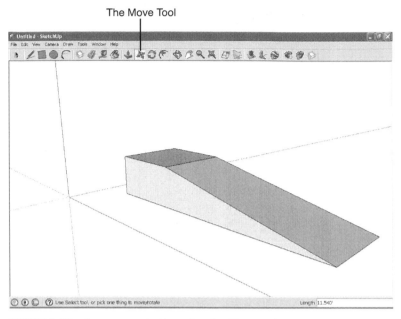

FIGURE 5.19   A ramp created by using the Move tool.

5. Select the **Move tool** in the toolbar (as shown in Figure 5.19).

6. Press the mouse button on the lower-right edge of the cube.

7. Drag the edge away from the cube to form the ramp. As you drag, the ramp extends from the cube.

8. Click the mouse at the location you want for the end of the ramp. When you do, the ramp becomes permanent (unless you erase it), as shown in Figure 5.19.

That's how the Move tool works in 3D. Using this tool, you can drag edges, not surfaces, into 3D, as in the case of making a ramp from a cube.

As its name implies, you can also use the Move tool to move individual objects around. Simply use the Select tool to select the object, and then move the object into place with the Move tool.

Drawing 3D by Subtracting Elements

You often draw 3D objects by subtracting elements. To show how this works, we'll draw a table like the one you see in Figure 5.20.

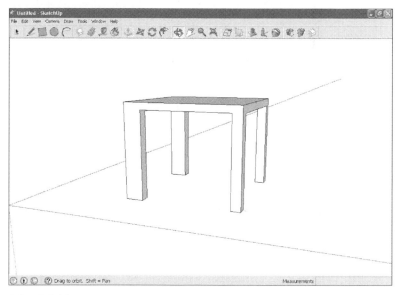

FIGURE 5.20 A 3D table.

How was that table created? Here's how:

1. Click the **Start Using SketchUp** button and click the human figure that appears in the Engineering–Feet template to select it; press the Del key to delete it.

2. Draw a horizontal rectangle.

3. Click the **Push/Pull tool** in the toolbar and move the mouse cursor to the rectangle.

4. Press the mouse button on the rectangle and drag the rectangle up to extend it into a 3D cube.

5. Select the **Rectangle tool** in the toolbar.

6. Draw a rectangle on the cube as shown in Figure 5.21.

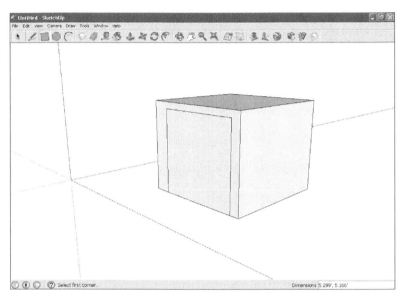

FIGURE 5.21   Adding a rectangle to a cube.

7. Select the **Push/Pull tool** in the toolbar.

8. Push the rectangle through the cube until you get a cutout in the shape of the rectangle.

9. Select the **Rectangle tool** in the toolbar.

10. Draw a rectangle on a cube surface adjacent to the first surface where you drew a rectangle. Draw the rectangle so that pushing it through will give you two of the table's legs.

11. Select the **Push/Pull** tool in the toolbar.

12. Push the rectangle through until you get a cutout in the shape of the rectangle. You can see what the result will look like in Figure 5.22.

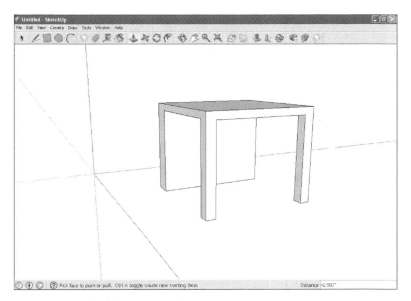

FIGURE 5.22   Pushing through a rectangle.

13. Select the **Rectangle tool** in the toolbar.

14. Draw a rectangle on the remaining vertical cube surface. Draw the rectangle so that pushing it through will give you the final two table legs.

15. Select the **Push/Pull tool** in the toolbar.

16. Push the rectangle through until you get a cutout in the shape of the rectangle. That creates the table in Figure 5.20.

And that's one technique for drawing 3D—by subtracting elements.

> TIP: **Making the Table Legs Identical**
>
> If you want to make sure the table legs are identical in all dimensions, you can use inferring. Select the Move tool, hover over the surface of a leg, then click another leg's corresponding surface to snap to the corresponding measurement.

LESSON 6

Creating Components and Groups

In this lesson, we're going to take the shapes we've been drawing in the previous lessons and start assembling them into groups and components to let us handle them all together.

Getting Started

For example, suppose that you've been drawing a car with all the surfaces you need for that. But then you find when you want to move or copy and rotate or even enlarge the model, you have to select all the surfaces individually to handle them all together.

Wouldn't it be easier to have SketchUp understand that it's supposed to treat all the surfaces of the car as a collection, handling all actions on all surfaces in the collection at once?

That's what groups and components are all about, and you'll find yourself using both of these as you progress in SketchUp. When you take shapes and/or objects and collect them into a group or component, you can then handle the collection of shapes as one object, copying it all at once, or moving, rotating it, and so on.

Many of the tools in SketchUp behave differently when you're working with a group or component than when you're just working with a Engineering–Feet shape, so we'll also discuss how that works in this lesson.

> NOTE: **What's the Difference Between Groups and Components?**
>
> It has to do with the fact that when you edit one component, all copies of the component are edited as well, but that's not true of groups.

Let's get started immediately by seeing how SketchUp handles multiple objects by default.

Using Sticky Geometry

We'll start this lesson with a discussion of the rudimentary way that SketchUp handles collections of objects by default—using a system called sticky geometry.

> NOTE: **On the Use of Tools**
>
> It's assumed in these tasks that you have been progressing through each lesson in order and learning about the individual tools referenced here. If you need to flip back for review, check out Lesson 3, "Drawing Shapes: Lines, Rectangles, Polygons, and Circles," for more on the Rectangle and Circle tools. And see Lesson 5, "Going 3D," for refreshers on the Push/Pull and Move tools.

When you bring two objects next to each other, they can "adhere" and become one object. It's sort of a rudimentary form of creating groups in SketchUp. Because sticky geometry is part of SketchUp, and because it's all about connecting objects into one (the topic of this lesson), we'll take a look at sticky geometry here.

To get an idea of how sticky geometry works, follow these steps:

1. Start SketchUp. For this task, we'll work with the Engineering–Feet template we've used in the previous lessons.

2. Click the **Start Using SketchUp** button.

3. Select the **Rectangle tool**.

4. Draw a horizontal rectangle.

5. Select the **Push/Pull tool** in the toolbar.

6. Pull the rectangle up into a cube.

7. Create a second cube, just as you did with the first cube.

8. Select the **Select tool** in the toolbar.

9. Draw a selection rectangle around the second cube.

10. Select the **Move tool** in the toolbar.

11. Move the cube until one surface touches a surface of the first cube.

12. Select the **Select tool** in the toolbar.

13. Draw a selection rectangle around the second cube.

14. Select the **Move tool** in the toolbar.

15. Move the second cube. If SketchUp has connected the cubes automatically through sticky geometry, you'll find that moving the second cube also pulls the first, as you see in Figure 6.1.

That's sticky geometry—it lets you connect objects by just putting them next to each other.

On the other hand, sticky geometry might not be right for you, because you might want a more systematic way of creating groups and components. For that reason, take a look at the following tasks.

Creating a Group

In this task, we'll take a look at the process of creating a group. When you create a group, you associate objects together, and tell SketchUp you want them all handled together. You can move them together, rotate them together, enlarge or reduce them together, and so on.

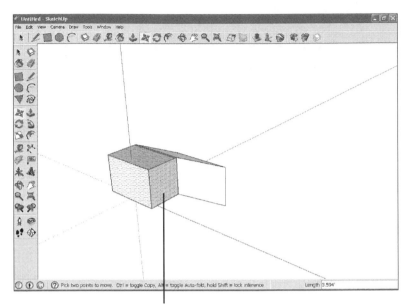

These objects are now grouped; if you grab and
move either, both move at the same time

FIGURE 6.1 Two cubes attached with sticky geometry.

Here we'll create a group from a cube and a cylinder. Here's how it works:

1. Click the **Start Using SketchUp** button and click the human fig-
    ure that appears in the Engineering–Feet template to select it;
    press the Del key to delete it.

2. Select the **Rectangle tool** and draw a horizontal rectangle.

3. Select the **Push/Pull tool** in the toolbar and then pull the rectan-
    gle up into a cube.

4. Select the **Circle tool** and draw a circle next to the cube, as
    shown in Figure 6.2.

5. Select the **Push/Pull tool** in the toolbar, and then pull the circle
    into a cylinder, as shown in Figure 6.3.

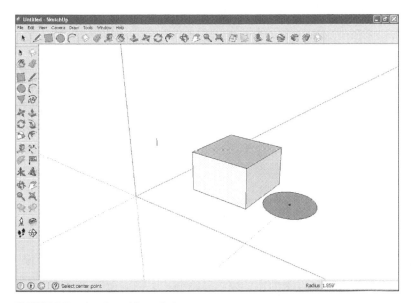

FIGURE 6.2 A cube with a circle.

6. Select the **Select tool**, and then, while holding down the left mouse button, draw a selection rectangle around both the cube and the cylinder.

7. Select the Edit menu's **Make Group** menu item. This creates a group of the cube and cylinder and selects that group, displaying it in a blue box, as shown in Figure 6.4.

NOTE: **Groups and Blue Boxes**

Groups aren't normally displayed with a blue box around them—the blue box appears only to indicate that the group is selected.

To prove this group functions now as a single unit, we'll move it around the screen.

1. Select the **Move tool** in the toolbar.

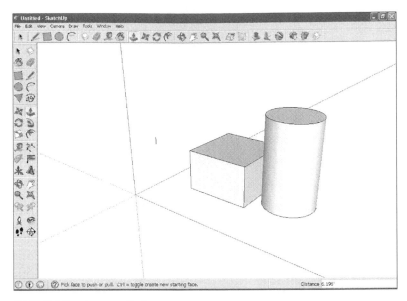

FIGURE 6.3   A new cylinder.

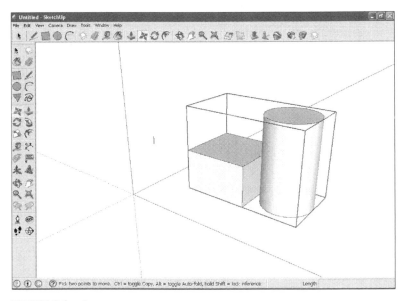

FIGURE 6.4   A new group.

2. Move the group to a new position, as shown in Figure 6.5.

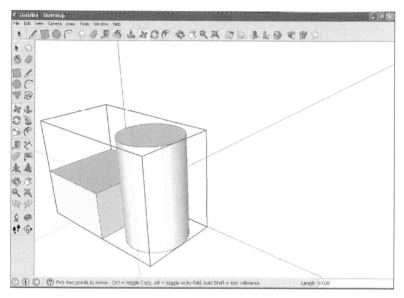

FIGURE 6.5 Moving the group.

3. When you move the group, both objects that make up the group move in unison, treated as a single object.

So now you've been able to group objects together and treat them as a group.

Creating Components

In this task, we'll create a component from the same two objects we saw in the previous task—a cube and a cylinder.

Here's how it works:

1. Click the **Start Using SketchUp** button and click the human figure that appears in the Engineering–Feet template to select it; press the Del key to delete it.

2. Select the **Rectangle tool** and draw a horizontal rectangle.

3. Select the **Push/Pull tool** in the toolbar, and then pull the rectangle up into a cube.

4. Select the **Circle tool** and draw a circle next to the cube.

5. Select the **Push/Pull tool** in the toolbar, and then pull the circle into a cylinder.

6. Select the **Select tool**, and then draw a selection rectangle around both the cube and the cylinder.

7. Select the Edit menu's **Make Component** menu item. SketchUp displays the dialog box you see in Figure 6.6.

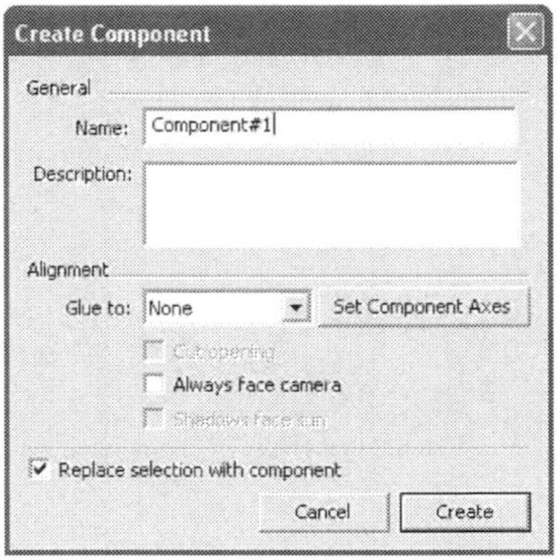

FIGURE 6.6   The Create Component dialog box.

8. Enter **Cube Cylinder Component** in the Name box.

9. Enter **A cube with a cylinder** in the Description box.

10. Click the **Create** button. The dialog box disappears and a blue selection box surrounds your new component, exactly as with the group in the previous task (refer to Figure 6.4).

To prove this component functions now as a single unit, we'll move it around the screen.

1. Select the **Move tool** in the toolbar.

2. Move the component to a new position, as shown in Figure 6.7.

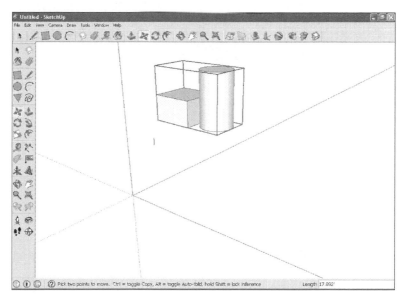

FIGURE 6.7 Moving the component.

3. When you move the component, both objects that make up the component move in unison, treated as a single unit.

Now you've created your first component. In the previous topic, you created your first group. What's the difference? See the next task.

Editing Components

You can also edit the various parts of a component in SketchUp.

In this task, we'll create a component from the same two objects we saw in the previous task—a cube and a cylinder.

Here's how it works:

1. Right-click the **Cube and Cylinder component** we created in the previous task.

2. Select the **Edit Component** menu item. This will surround the component with a dotted box, as shown in Figure 6.8.

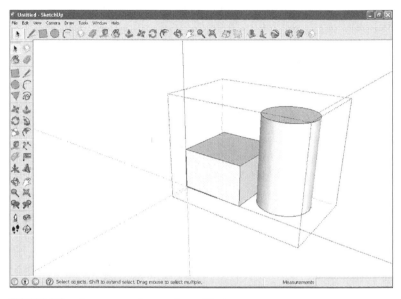

FIGURE 6.8   A component open for editing.

3. Select the **Push/Pull tool** in the toolbar.

4. Hover over the top surface of the rectangle for two seconds.

5. Click the top surface of the cylinder to pull the cube up to match the cylinder in height, as you see in Figure 6.9. This is sizing the cube by inference.

6. Select the **Select tool** in the toolbar.

7. Click any blank, nonselected region of the screen to stop editing the component. The dotted box around the component disappears.

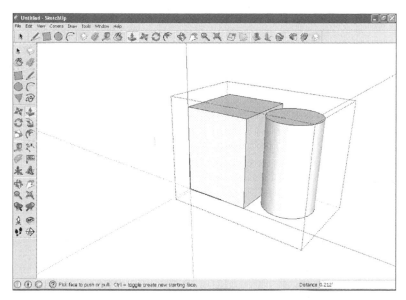

FIGURE 6.9   An edited component.

That's it—now you know how to edit the individual objects in a component.

Understanding the Difference Between Groups and Components

Now you've seen groups and components. What's the difference?

The difference is that components are *instanced*. That's a SketchUp term meaning that all copies of a component act as instances of—or are tied to—the original. Thus, if you make a copy of a component and edit it, both the copy and the original will be affected, which is not true for groups.

When you make a copy of a group, the copy is totally independent of the original. That means that if you edit a group, no copies of the group will be affected.

Let's take a look at how components work when you edit one of a set of the same component:

1. Start SketchUp.

2. Click the **Start Using SketchUp** button. This will open SketchUp.

3. Select the **Select tool** in the toolbar.

4. Click the **Cube and Cylinder component** that we have created in this lesson. This selects the component, surrounding it with a blue box.

   Now we'll make a copy of the component.

5. Select the Edit menu's **Copy** item.

6. Select the Edit menu's **Paste** item.

7. Move the mouse to the location at which you want to place the copy of the component.

8. Click the mouse to create a copy of the component. Now you have an original and a copy of the component on the screen.

9. Right-click one of the Cube and Cylinder components.

10. Select the **Edit Component** menu item. This will surround the component with a dotted box, as shown in Figure 6.10.

11. Select the **Push/Pull tool** in the toolbar.

12. Pull the cylinder up to a greater height. As you pull the cylinder in one component, the cylinder in the other component changes to match, as shown in Figure 6.11.

13. Select the **Select tool** in the toolbar.

14. Click any blank, nonselected region of the screen to stop editing the component. The dotted box around the component disappears.

There you have it—when you edit one object in a component, that same change is made to the corresponding object in all copies of the component (which doesn't happen when you make copies of groups).

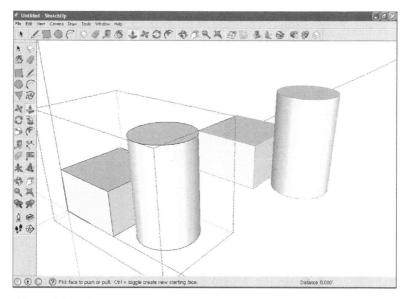

FIGURE 6.10   A component ready for editing.

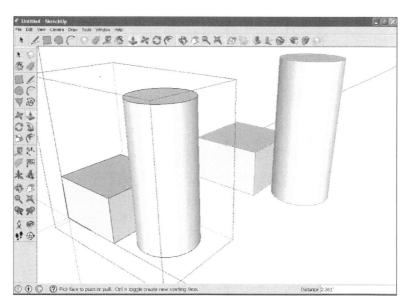

FIGURE 6.11   Editing a component, which also edits copies of the component.

Exploding a Component

Having created a component, can you de-create it? That is, can you "explode" the objects in the component so that they no longer make up a component?

Yes, you can. Just follow these steps to create a component and then explode it back into its parts:

1. Click the **Start Using SketchUp** button and click the human figure that appears in the Engineering–Feet template to select it; press the Del key to delete it.

2. Select the **Rectangle tool** and draw a horizontal rectangle.

3. Select the **Push/Pull tool** in the toolbar, and then pull the rectangle up into a cube.

4. Select the **Circle tool** and draw a circle next to the cube.

5. Select the **Push/Pull tool** in the toolbar, and then pull the circle into a cylinder.

6. Select the **Select tool**, and then draw a selection rectangle around both the cube and the cylinder.

7. Select the Edit menu's **Make Component** item. SketchUp displays a dialog box.

8. Enter **Two Cubes Component** in the Name box.

9. Enter **Two cubes** in the Description box.

10. Click the **Create** button. The dialog box disappears.

    A blue selection box surrounds your new component—you've created your component.

    The next step is to explode it back into two separate cubes.

11. While your component is selected (has a blue box around it), right-click the component. A context menu appears.

12. Select **Explode** from the context menu. The blue selection box around the component disappears, and the two cubes are no longer one component.

To verify that the two cubes are separate, click them individually, noting that no blue box appears—instead, first one cube then the other is filled with blue dots, as happens when you select individual objects.

Now you know how to create and "uncreate" components.

Managing Components

SketchUp includes a utility to manage your components, and we'll take a look at it in this task.

Here's how it works:

1. Start SketchUp. For this task, we'll work with the Engineering–Feet template we've used in the previous tasks.

2. Click the **Start Using SketchUp** button.

3. Select the Window menu's **Components** item. This will open the Components dialog box you see in Figure 6.12. (I've used the mouse to enlarge the Components dialog, dragging one corner, to make what's going on in the dialog box clearer.)

FIGURE 6.12   The Component dialog box.

4. To see the components you have in the current model, click the down arrow next to the house button, and select the **In Model** item. This will display the page you see in Figure 6.13.

FIGURE 6.13   The current component in the model.

Because the only component in the model currently is the human figure that SketchUp shows on startup, that's the only component (named Susan in SketchUp 8) that appears in the dialog box when you ask to see all the components in the current model.

5. To insert an instance of a component into your model, click that component. Doing so makes the component instance appear at the location of the mouse cursor.

6. To place the component instance in your model, just move the mouse to the location at which you want the component to appear, and click it. The component becomes anchored to the location of the mouse click.

That's it—that's one way to manage your components. Take a look at the next task for another.

Using the Component Sampler

SketchUp also has a "Sampler" of prebuilt components available for you to use. Here's how it works:

1. Start SketchUp. For this task, we'll work with the Engineering–Feet template we've used in the previous tasks.

2. Click the **Start Using SketchUp** button.

3. Select the Window menu's **Components** item. This will open the Components dialog box.

   By default, you should see the Component Sampler. Click it to open it, as shown in Figure 6.14. (If you don't see the **Components Sampler**, click the down arrow next to the house icon to select it.)

FIGURE 6.14   The Component dialog showing the Component Sampler.

4. Scroll up and down the Component Sampler to get an idea of what's available.

5. To insert an instance of a component into your model, click that component. Doing so makes the component instance appear at the location of the mouse cursor.

6. To place the component instance in your model, move the mouse to the location at which you want the component to appear, and click it. The component becomes anchored to the location of the mouse click.

Using the 3D Warehouse

SketchUp also has available a "warehouse" of components that you can use and download.

Let's assume you want to draw a couch. Here's how it works:

1. Click the **Start Using SketchUp** button.

2. Select the Window menu's **Components** item. This opens the Components dialog box. By default, you should see the Component Sampler.

3. Click the down arrow next to the house button. This will display a drop-down menu of component collections.

The choices for the Component collections are

▶ Architecture

▶ Landscape

▶ Construction

▶ People

▶ Playground

▶ Transportation

For this task, we'll choose the Architecture collections.

4. Select the **Architecture** menu item. This will display a dialog box, as you see in Figure 6.15, of component collections available in Google's 3D Warehouse.

5. Select the **Furniture** item. This displays the items in the Furniture collection of Google's 3D warehouse, as shown in Figure 6.16.

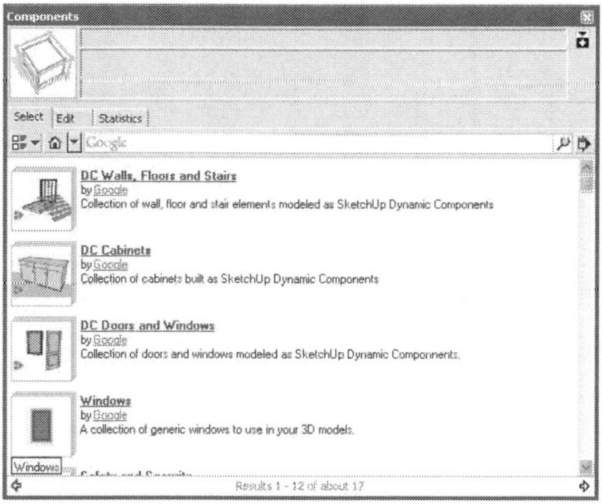

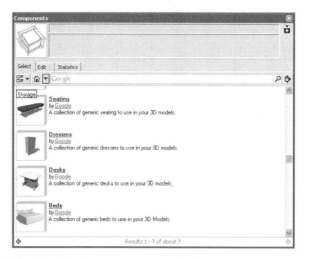

FIGURE 6.15   The Architecture component collections.

FIGURE 6.16   The Furniture component collections.

6. Click the **Seating** item. This downloads the Seating collection from the 3D warehouse, as shown in Figure 6.17.

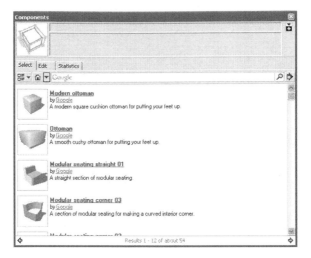

FIGURE 6.17   The Seating component collections.

7. Click the **Couch Rounded** item. Doing so makes the component instance appear at the location of the mouse cursor.

8. To place the component instance in your model, move the mouse to the location at which you want the component to appear, and click it. The component becomes anchored to the location of the mouse click, as shown in Figure 6.18.

There are dozens of components ready for you to download and use from the 3D warehouse—give it a try.

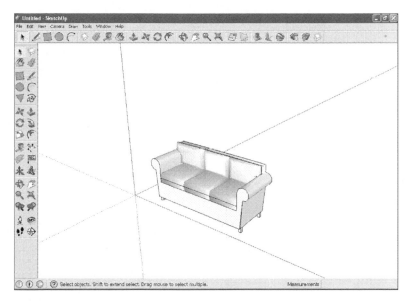

FIGURE 6.18 A new couch.

LESSON 7

Painting Your Objects

So far, we've been drawing objects using the SketchUp default shading, but that's probably not what you have in mind to color your own objects. You can also paint your objects.

Painting

For example, take a look at Figure 7.1, where you can see a cube of wood.

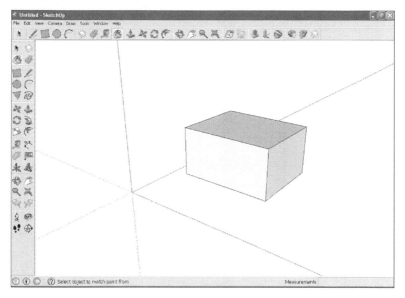

FIGURE 7.1 A cube.

Or is it? It certainly doesn't look like a cube of wood. Now take a look at Figure 7.2, where we've used the Paint tool (the tool with the paint bucket icon) and painted the block with a wood texture—if you can see the grain on the various faces, you can see that it looks a lot more like a block of wood.

The Paint Tool

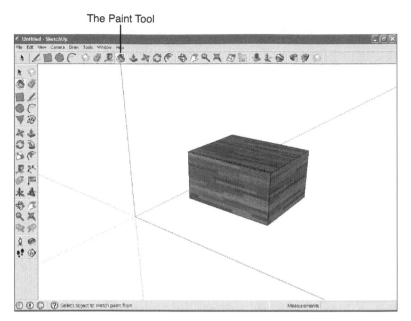

FIGURE 7.2 A block of wood created using the Paint tool.

That's what painting looks like in SketchUp. You don't usually just paint colors, you paint textures, too. SketchUp comes with a large selection of textures for you to paint with—everything from wood to brick.

TIP: **Texture Aligns with Surfaces**

In addition, it's worth noting that the textures you paint align with the surface. That means, for example, that when you paint a surface to have a wood texture, the grain of the wood aligns with the surface.

Let's get started.

Using the Paint Tool

In the first task for this lesson, we'll see how to use the paint bucket at its simplest, just bringing it up and painting some surfaces.

To get started with the Paint tool, follow these steps:

1. Start SketchUp. The Welcome to SketchUp dialog box appears. For this task, we'll work with the Engineering–Feet template we've used in the previous lessons.

2. Click the **Start Using SketchUp** button.

3. Select the **Rectangle tool**.

4. Draw a horizontal rectangle.

5. Select the **Push/Pull tool** in the toolbar.

6. Pull the rectangle up into a cube.

7. Select the **Paint tool** in the toolbar (refer to Figure 7.2).

    Selecting the Paint tool displays the materials browser, as shown in Figure 7.3.

    The materials browser lets you select the material you want to paint with. By default, the materials browser will have a texture selected, such as brick.

8. Click all surfaces of the cube. This will paint all surfaces of the cube with the texture selected in the materials browser.

    If you like, you can orbit and paint the back surfaces as well.

    You can see the results in Figure 7.4, where the cube has been painted with brick texture.

That lets us get started with painting. But the default texture that SketchUp selected is probably not what you had in mind to paint that car or chair you've been drawing.

To see how to set your own textures, take a look at the next task.

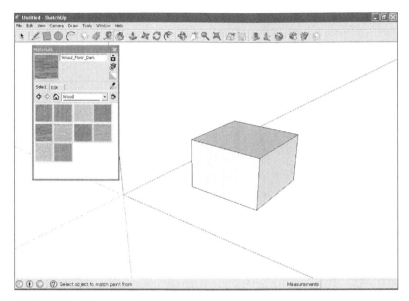

FIGURE 7.3   The materials browser.

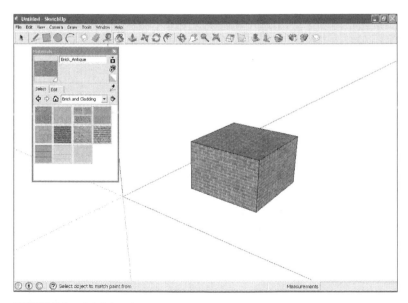

FIGURE 7.4   A brick cube.

Selecting Materials

Let's say you want to draw a tile floor. How would you select that texture to paint it?

Follow these steps:

1. Click the **Start Using SketchUp** button.

2. Select the **Rectangle tool** in the toolbar.

3. Draw a horizontal rectangle.

4. Select the **Paint tool** in the toolbar.

    The materials browser opens. You can select a collection of textures from the drop-down texture list box (next to the button displaying a house). Then you can choose from the following texture collections:

    ► Carpet and textiles
    ► Colors
    ► Colors–Named
    ► Fencing
    ► Groundcover
    ► Markers
    ► Metal
    ► Roofing
    ► Sketchy
    ► Stone
    ► Tile
    ► Translucent
    ► Vegetation
    ► Water
    ► Wood

5. Select the Tile texture collection from the textures drop-down list.

6. Select a tile texture of your liking by clicking it.

7. Click the horizontal rectangle. The rectangle is painted in the texture you've requested, as shown in Figure 7.5.

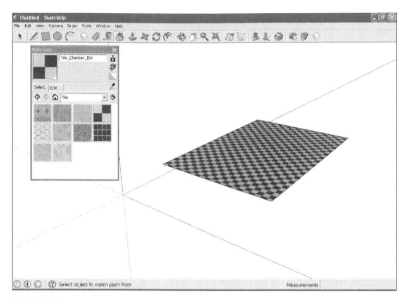

FIGURE 7.5   A tile floor.

There you have it—now you're drawing with textures.

Eliminating Automatic Shading

You might have noticed that SketchUp automatically shades the objects it draws. So, for example, the top of the cube in Figure 7.1 appears dark compared to the cube's sides. However, now that you're setting your own textures and painting objects, you may prefer that SketchUp not shade objects automatically. For example, that tile floor in Figure 7.5 appears dark because of automatic shading.

To eliminate automatic shading, follow these steps:

1. Click the **Start Using SketchUp** button. This opens SketchUp.

2. Select the Window menu's **Shadow** item. This opens the Shadow Settings dialog box you see in the upper left of Figure 7.6.

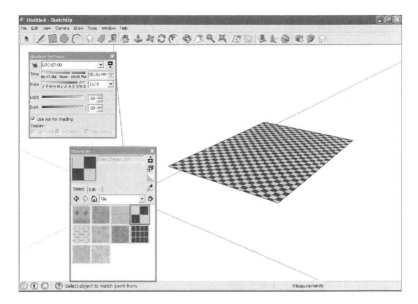

FIGURE 7.6 The Shadow Settings dialog box.

3. Set both the Light and Dark settings to 100.

4. Click the **X** button at the upper right to close the Shadow Settings dialog box.

Now the tile floor created in the previous task is not automatically shaded, as you can see in Figure 7.6.

TIP: **Using the Sun for Shading**

You can also simulate the sun for your shading needs. Simply select the Use Sun for Shading check box in the Shadow Settings dialog box.

Drawing in Solid Color

Let's say you wanted a pink circle. That's it, just a plain pink circle. No texture, just plain color. How would you get it?

Here's how (note that figures are grayscale only):

1. Click the **Start Using SketchUp** button.

2. Select the **Circle tool** in the toolbar.

3. Draw a horizontal circle.

4. Select the **Paint tool** in the toolbar.

    The materials browser opens.

5. Select the **Colors** texture collection from the textures drop-down list. The materials browser displays many colors, as you can see in Figure 7.7.

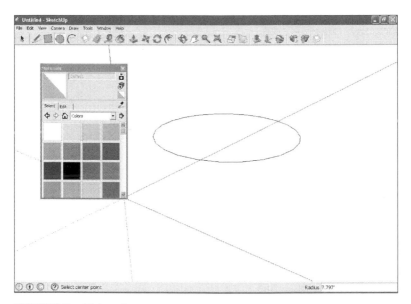

FIGURE 7.7   Plain colors.

6. Scroll up and down through the colors until you find a shade of pink you like.

7. Click the horizontal circle. The circles are painted plain pink, as shown in Figure 7.8.

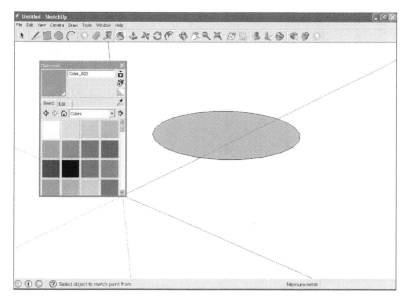

FIGURE 7.8   A pink circle.

TIP: **Selecting Named Colors**

Want to choose your colors by name, such as cyan, magenta, coral, and so on? Just select Colors–Named in the textures drop-down list and let the mouse hover over the color rectangles. A ToolTip will appear showing the name of the color you're hovering over.

Painting Multiple Surfaces at Once

You can paint multiple surfaces at once, which is great if you're trying to select from among different textures and want to try them all, but don't want to have to click every surface each time you select a different texture.

Here's how it works:

1. Click the **Start Using SketchUp** button.

2. Select the **Circle tool**.

3. Draw three horizontal circles.

4. Select the **Select tool** in the toolbar.

5. Holding down the Ctrl key (Option key on the Mac), click all three circles to select them.

6. Select the **Paint tool** in the toolbar.

   The materials browser opens.

7. Select the texture collection you want from the textures drop-down list.

8. Select a texture of your liking by clicking it.

9. Click a horizontal circle. When you do, all three circles are painted at the same time, as you see in Figure 7.9.

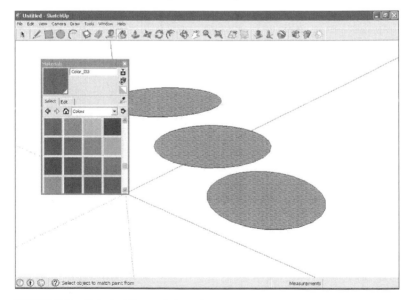

FIGURE 7.9   Coloring three circles at once.

Now you're able to paint multiple surfaces at once.

Examining All Materials in Your Model

Want to take a look at all the textures in your model at once?

You can do that in SketchUp. To see how, let's draw a cube, add textures to its various faces, and then take a look at the textures in the drawing all at once. Here's how it works:

1. Click the **Start Using SketchUp** button.

2. Select the **Rectangle tool**.

3. Draw a horizontal rectangle.

4. Select the **Push/Pull tool** in the toolbar.

5. Pull the rectangle up into a cube.

6. Select the **Paint tool** in the toolbar.

   Selecting the Paint tool displays the materials browser.

7. Select a texture collection you like. In this example, we're going to use the first collection in the Texture drop-down list box, the Bricks and Cladding collection.

8. Select a texture by clicking it.

9. Click a face of the cube to give it that texture.

10. Repeat steps 8 and 9 for all visible faces of the cube.

11. Click the **Home** button in the materials browser. This will display all the textures currently in the drawing, as you can see in Figure 7.10.

TIP: **Too Many Textures?**

Why are there more textures displayed in the materials browser than you painted on the cube? The answer is that the template

---

we're using, Engineering–Feet, comes with several built-in plain color textures to create the human figure that originally appears when SketchUp starts.

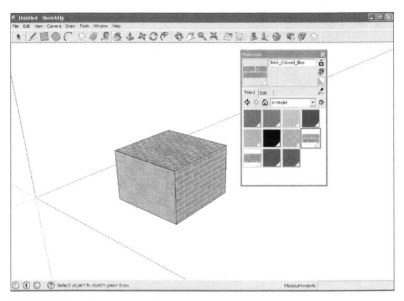

FIGURE 7.10   The textures in our drawing.

That's it—now you know how to access all the textures in your drawing.

> TIP: **More Details for Your Textures**
>
> To see the name of the textures in your drawing, hover the mouse over them in the materials browser and the texture's name will appear in a ToolTip. For solid colors, the RGB values (that is, the red, green, and blue values with a range of 0–255) appear separated by commas in the ToolTip, such as: 96, 96, 96.

Creating Materials

What if you can't find the material you're looking for in the materials browser? What if your material doesn't seem to exist yet?

You can create your own. Just follow these steps:

1. Click the **Start Using SketchUp** button.

2. Select the **Paint tool** in the toolbar.

   Selecting the Paint tool displays the materials browser.

3. Click the **Create Material** button in the materials browser. The Create Material button is the second button from the top on the right of the materials browser. Clicking it opens the Create Material dialog box, as shown in Figure 7.11.

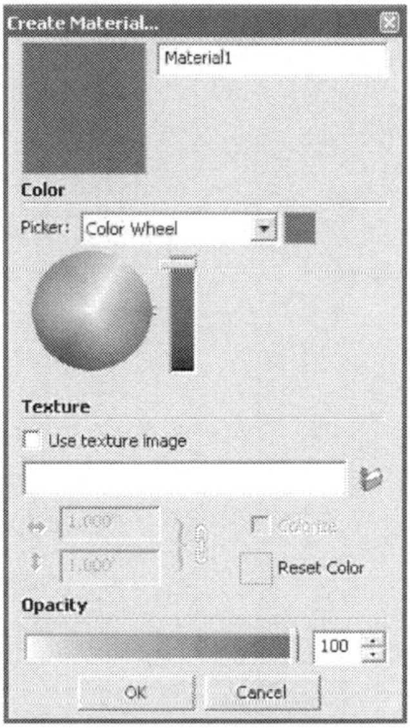

FIGURE 7.11   The Create Material dialog box.

In this example, we'll make a new material from a solid color.

4. Enter a name for your new material. In this example, we'll leave the name Material1, the default name for the new material.

5. Click a location in the color wheel. The square at the top left in the Create Material dialog box changes to display that color.

6. Click the **OK** button. The Create Material dialog box closes, and
your new material is added to the In Model collection of textures,
as shown in Figure 7.12.

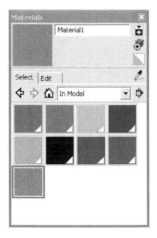

FIGURE 7.12   A new material.

Now you can use your new material to paint with as you like.

> NOTE: **Images as Textures**
> You can also use any saved image for the texture of the material
> you want to create. Just click the Use Texture Image check box in
> the Create Material dialog box, and browse to find the image file
> you want to use as your new texture.

Editing Materials

Want to edit a material you've created? Just follow these steps:

1. Click the **Start Using SketchUp** button.

2. Select the **Paint tool** in the toolbar.

   Selecting the Paint tool displays the materials browser.

3. Click the **Home** button (the button displaying a house) to display
the materials in your model.

4. Select a material by clicking it. This opens the materials in your model, as shown in Figure 7.13.

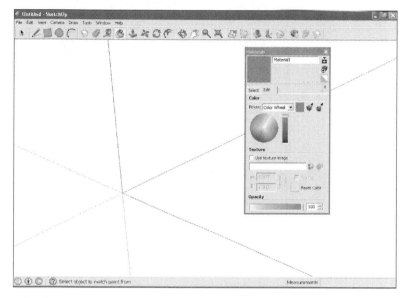

FIGURE 7.13 Editing a material.

5. Click a new location in the color wheel, if desired. The square at the top left in the Create Material dialog box changes to display that color.

6. Click the Use Texture Image check box to change the image for the material's texture.

7. Browse to the image file that holds the image you want to use for texture and select it; then click Open in the browsing dialog box.

8. Click the **Select** tab. The edits you made to your material will be saved automatically.

In this way, you can make any changes to materials.

Replacing All of a Material in a Drawing

Take a look at the cubes in Figure 7.14, all surfaces of which are painted with bricks.

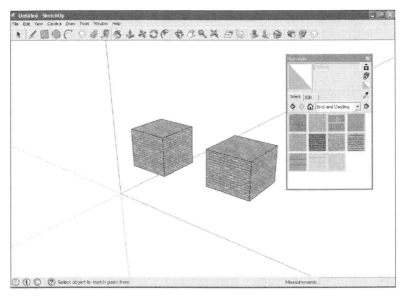

FIGURE 7.14   Two cubes with painted faces.

What if you wanted to change the material used to paint the cubes to, say, wood? Do you have to click each face of each cube individually?

No—you can change all occurrences of a material in a drawing at once with SketchUp. In this task, we'll draw the two cubes and then change their materials from brick to wood. Here's how it works:

1. Click the **Start Using SketchUp** button.

2. Select the **Rectangle tool** and draw a horizontal rectangle.

3. Select the **Push/Pull tool** in the toolbar and pull the rectangle up into a cube.

4. Repeat steps 2 and 3 to draw the second cube.

5. Select the **Paint tool** in the toolbar.

Selecting the Paint tool displays the materials browser.

6. Select the **Bricks and Cladding** texture collection in the materials browser.

7. Select the Concrete Block (that is, large gray brick) texture in the Bricks and Cladding collection by clicking it.

8. Click all surfaces of the cubes. This will paint all surfaces of the cube with the concrete blocks.

Now we'll change the material used in the cubes to wood.

9. Select the **Wood** texture collection in the materials browser.

10. Select the wood texture you like best by clicking it.

11. Hold down the Shift key.

12. Click one surface of a cube. When you do, all surfaces painted with the same material change to the wood texture you've selected.

You can see the results in Figure 7.15, where the cubes have been painted with wood texture.

As you can see, it's simple to repaint an object.

TIP: **Painting Adjacent Surfaces**
You can also restrict the repainting to adjacent surfaces if you use the Ctrl (Option key on the Mac) instead of the Shift key.

Sampling Existing Materials

If you open a drawing that has materials unfamiliar to you, you can sample those materials and see if SketchUp can figure out what the name of the textures are.

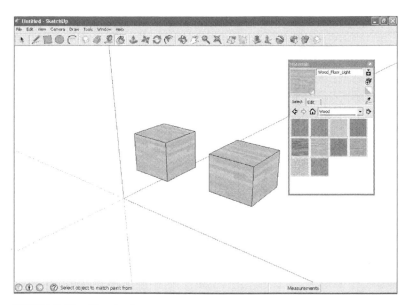

FIGURE 7.15   Wood cubes.

For example, in this task, we'll draw a cube with bricks on it, then sample the material used to paint the surface and confirm that it's brick. Here's how it works:

1. Click the **Start Using SketchUp** button.

2. Select the **Rectangle tool** and draw a horizontal rectangle.

3. Select the **Push/Pull tool** in the toolbar and pull the rectangle up into a cube.

4. Select the **Paint tool** in the toolbar.

    Selecting the Paint tool displays the materials browser.

5. Select the **Bricks and Cladding** texture collection in the materials browser.

6. Select a brick texture that you like by clicking it.

7. Click all surfaces of the cube. This will paint all surfaces of the cube with brick.

Now we'll sample a cube surface and see if SketchUp can determine what the material is.

8. Select the **Dropper** button in the materials browser. The mouse cursor changes to a dropper image.

9. Click a surface of the cube. SketchUp will determine which material the dropper has clicked and display that material, as well as its name, in the square at the upper left in the materials browser, as you can see in Figure 7.16.

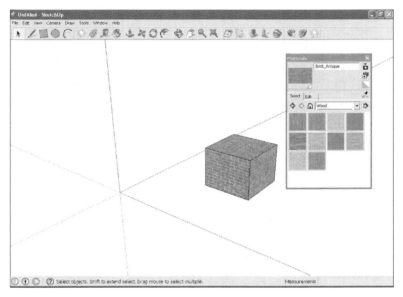

FIGURE 7.16   Sampling materials.

It can be very useful to sample materials in this way to determine just what materials they are.

Undoing Changes and Canceling Operations

Paint a surface and then wish you hadn't? SketchUp can undo the change.

In fact, nearly every operation you perform in SketchUp can be undone; from drawing a line to painting a surface, or even deleting an object.

To undo an operation, select the Edit menu's Undo item. The operation will be undone and the drawing will be restored to its previous condition. You can also press Ctrl + Z (Option + Z on the Mac) to do the same thing.

What if you've started an operation and want to cancel it? For example, suppose you started drawing a line and then changed your mind, but the Line tool is still stretching a line from the point you clicked to the present mouse location as you move the mouse.

Just press the Esc key. That cancels any operation that you've started and gets you out of it.

Using the Rotate, Scale, and Follow-Me Tools

In this lesson, we're going to gain more SketchUp power by manipulating objects.

Using Some New Tools

Here, we'll learn to use the Rotate, Scale, and Follow-Me tools.

- ▶ The Rotate tool does just what it sounds like—it rotates objects. You can use this tool not only to rotate whole objects, but also parts of objects if you select a part of the object and then fold it across edges.

- ▶ The Scale tool lets you enlarge and reduce objects as you like. This is a useful tool in case you want to make changes to an object's size at any time.

- ▶ The Follow-Me tool lets you move 2D shapes along paths you've specified to create 3D shapes. It's very cool to watch.

Let's get started with the Rotate tool.

Rotating Objects

The Rotate tool lets you rotate whole objects, or just part of an object.

The Rotate tool first establishes a plane of rotation by orienting itself to the planes formed by the red, blue, and green axes, or any surface you hover over. Then you establish an axis of rotation and rotate the object.

First, we'll need an object to rotate. We'll use the Components dialog (as we did in Lesson 6, "Creating Components and Groups") and bring forth a workstation desk set and orient it the way we want. For this task (and others in this lesson), we'll work with the familiar Engineering–Feet template.

Here's how we can rotate a drawing of a workstation:

1. Start SketchUp.

2. Click the **Start Using SketchUp** button.

3. Select the Window menu's **Components** item.

4. Click the down arrow next to the House button and click the **Architecture** component collection.

5. In the Architecture collection, click the **Furniture** collection.

6. In the Furniture collection, click the **Desks** collection.

7. Click the **Work Station Desk Set** component.

8. Click inside your drawing to draw the desk set, as shown in Figure 8.1. Now we'll rotate the desk set.

9. Select the **Rotate** tool in the toolbar (shown in Figure 8.1). Selecting the Rotate tool displays a rotation base, which appears as a double circle, at the location of the mouse cursor. As you move the mouse, SketchUp aligns the rotation base with the underlying surfaces.

10. Click the location under the desk around which you want to rotate the desk. This anchors the rotation base and sets the location around which you will rotate the object. You can think of the rotation base as an axle hub for the rotation.

> NOTE: **The Blue Box Indicates What Will Be Rotated**
>
> Note that because of the proximity of the rotation base and the desk, SketchUp surrounds the desk in a blue box to indicate that it has been selected as the target of your rotation operations.

The Rotate Tool

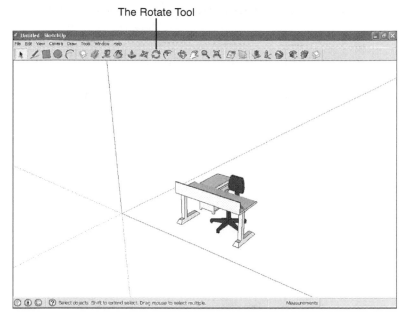

FIGURE 8.1 The Rotate tool and our desk.

11. After setting the rotation hub, you need to set the rotation axis, the axle around which the rotation will take place. Move the mouse to the end point of the rotation axis. One end point of the rotation axis is automatically the rotation base; the other you set by moving the mouse and then clicking it. The rotation axis is the axis, or axle, around which the rotation will take place.

12. Click the mouse to lock the rotation axis in place. You can see the rotation base and rotation axis we're using in Figure 8.2. Now you have the rotation base (the rotation axle hub) and the rotation axis (the rotation axle) in place. When you move the mouse, the desk rotates to match.

13. Move the mouse to rotate the object. This rotates the selected object in 3D space to follow the movements of the mouse.

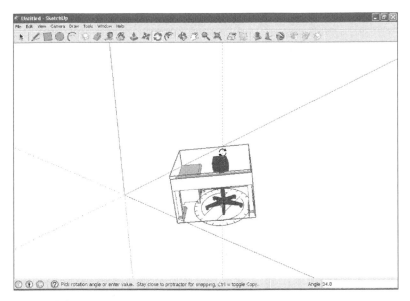

FIGURE 8.2   A rotation base and rotation axis.

14. Click the mouse to lock the object in its rotated position. You can see the new position of the desk in our example in Figure 8.3.

That's how rotation works in SketchUp.

Rotating Parts of Objects

The Rotate tool lets you rotate part of an object as well, which is great when you want to "fold" part of an object over.

For example, we'll rotate just part of a cube.

Here's how it works:

1. Click the **Start Using SketchUp** button.

2. Select the **Rectangle tool** and draw a horizontal rectangle.

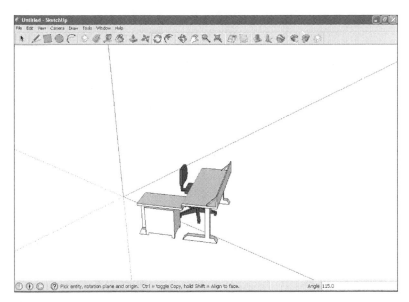

FIGURE 8.3   A rotated object.

3. Select the **Push/Pull tool** in the toolbar and pull the rectangle up into a cube.

4. Select the **Line tool** in the toolbar.

5. Draw a vertical line on one edge of the cube, as shown in Figure 8.4. Note that when you're drawing the line, it will turn cyan until it's parallel to the vertical edges of the cube. This is a useful guide if you want to draw a vertical line.

6. Now we'll rotate part of the cube around the vertical line. Choose the **Select tool** in the toolbar.

7. Click the right half of the bisected cube face. This selects that half of the cube face and fills it with blue dots to indicate that it has been selected.

8. Select the **Rotate tool** in the toolbar.

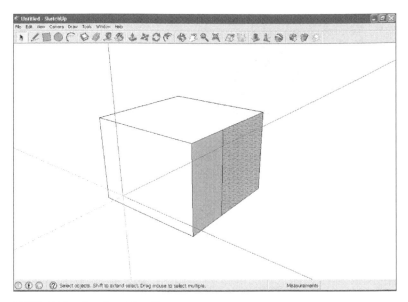

FIGURE 8.4   A cube with a line.

9. Click the location under the cube around which you want to rotate the selected part of the cube. That is, click directly under the bottom end point of the bisecting line.

10. After setting the rotation hub, you need to set the rotation axis, the axle around which the rotation will take place. Move the mouse to the end point of the rotation axis. That is, move the mouse directly above the top end point of the bisecting line.

NOTE: **One End Becomes the Rotation Axis**

One end point of the rotation axis is automatically the rotation base; the other you set by moving the mouse and then clicking it. The rotation axis is the axis, or axle, around which the rotation will take place.

---

11. Click the mouse to lock the rotation axis in place. Now you have the rotation base (the rotation axle hub) and the rotation axis (the rotation axle) in place. When you move the mouse, the desk will rotate to match.

12. Move the mouse to rotate the object. This rotates the selected object in 3D space to follow the movements of the mouse.

13. Click the mouse to lock the object in its rotated position. You can see the new position of the right half of the bisected cube face in our example in Figure 8.5.

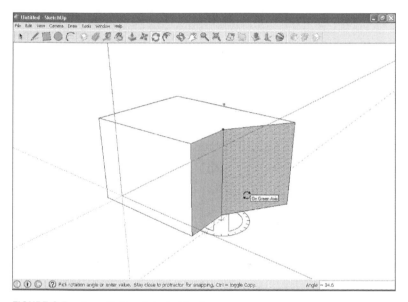

FIGURE 8.5 A partially rotated object.

Now you can partially rotate objects in SketchUp.

TIP: **You Can Also Use the Move Tool**

You can get the same effect as you see in Figure 8.5 with the Move tool if you drag the right-most edge of the cube forward.

Locking the Rotate Tool's Orientation

It's sometimes hard to get the Rotate tool's rotation base to use the orientation you want, because it aligns to any underlying surface. And if you have a complex object, what you consider the current underlying surface is not what SketchUp might consider the current underlying surface, which can be frustrating.

One trick you can use is to lock the rotation base's plane over a surface you like and then move it to the surface you're having problems with. When you lock the rotation base, it preserves its orientation no matter how what the underlying surface is.

Here's how it works:

1. Click the **Start Using SketchUp** button.

2. Select the **Rectangle tool** and draw a horizontal rectangle.

3. Select the **Push/Pull tool** in the toolbar and pull the rectangle up into a cube.

4. Select the **Rotate tool** in the toolbar.

5. Move the rotation base around the various surfaces and planes in the drawing to confirm that the rotation base aligns with the underlying surface. You can see examples in Figures 8.6 and 8.7.

6. Now we'll lock the rotation base in the horizontal position. Move the rotation base to an empty part of the drawing. By default, the rotation base takes a horizontal alignment.

7. Press the **Shift** key. Pressing the Shift key locks the orientation of the rotation base.

8. With the Shift key down, move the rotation base around the various surfaces and planes in the drawing to confirm that the rotation base stays horizontal. You can see examples in Figures 8.8 and 8.9.

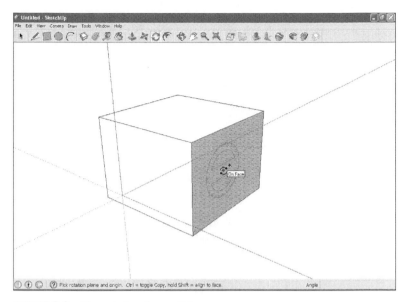

FIGURE 8.6   The rotation base aligns one way.

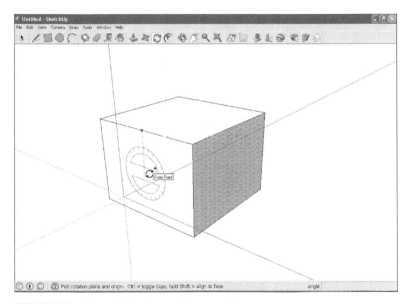

FIGURE 8.7   The rotation base aligns another way.

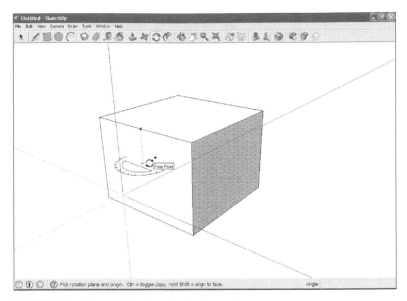

FIGURE 8.8   The rotation base is horizontal.

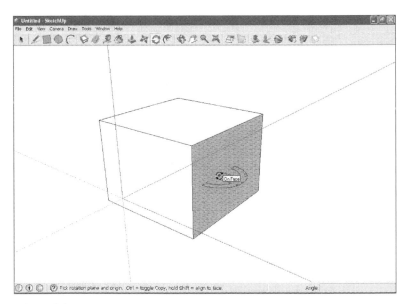

FIGURE 8.9   The rotation base stays horizontal.

There you have it—now you can keep the rotation base the way you want it.

Scaling 2D Objects

You can use the Scale tool to enlarge or reduce objects in SketchUp. Here's how the Scale tool works for 2D objects:

1. Click the **Start Using SketchUp** button.

2. Select the **Rectangle** tool and draw a horizontal rectangle.

3. Select the View menu's **Toolbars** item. This opens a submenu.

4. Select the submenu's **Large Tool Set** item. This opens the large toolbar.

5. Select the **Scale tool** in the large toolbar. The Scale tool is the tool that displays an image of a rectangle being expanded.

6. Click the horizontal rectangle. The rectangle has sizing handles added to it, as you can see in Figure 8.10.

7. Press the mouse button on a sizing handle. The sizing handle you choose determines how the rectangle will be stretched when you move the mouse, just as when you resize a window.

8. Drag the mouse to stretch the rectangle in the direction you've chosen. The rectangle stretches as you pull it.

9. Release the mouse button. When you do, the rectangle is fixed in place at its new size, as shown in Figure 8.11.

That's all it takes to resize objects—just use the Scale tool.

TIP: **Stretching Objects in Different Directions**

Note that if you pull one of the corner sizing handles, the object will be scaled so that it retains its proportions in both dimensions. But if you pull on an edge sizing handle, not a corner one, the object will be pulled in only the corresponding dimension, deforming the object.

The Scale Tool

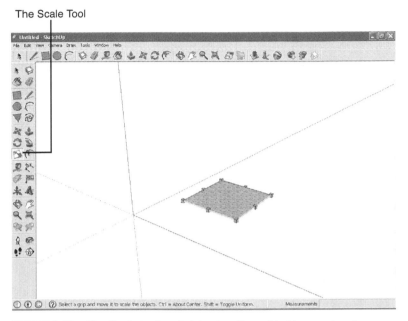

FIGURE 8.10   The Scale tool and sizing handles added to a rectangle.

Scaling 3D Objects

As you'd expect because SketchUp is a 3D program, you can also scale objects in 3D. To see this in action, we'll draw a cube and then scale it to make it bigger.

Here's how it works:

1. Click the **Start Using SketchUp** button.

2. Select the **Rectangle tool** and draw a horizontal rectangle.

3. Select the **Push/Pull tool** in the toolbar and pull the rectangle up into a cube.

4. Select the **Select tool** in the toolbar.

5. Draw a selection rectangle around the cube with the mouse.

6. Release the mouse button. When you do, the cube is selected.

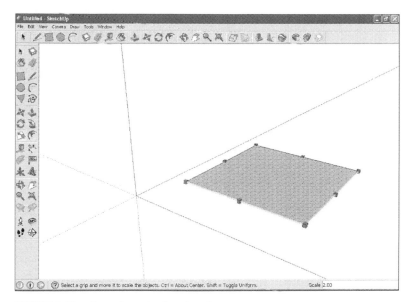

FIGURE 8.11 A newly resized rectangle.

7. Select the View menu's **Toolbars** item. This opens a submenu.

8. Select the submenu's **Large Tool Set** item. This opens the large toolbar.

9. Select the **Scale tool** in the large toolbar.

When you select the Scale tool, the cube has sizing handles added to it, as you can see in Figure 8.12.

10. Press the mouse button on a sizing handle. The sizing handle you choose determines how the cube will be stretched.

11. Drag the mouse to stretch the cube in the direction you've chosen. The cube stretches as you pull it.

12. Release the mouse button. When you do, the cube is fixed in place at its new size, as shown in Figure 8.13.

Now you can resize objects in 3D.

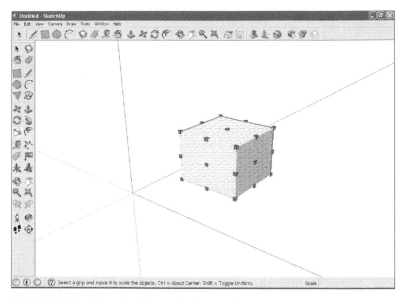

FIGURE 8.12   Sizing handles added to a cube.

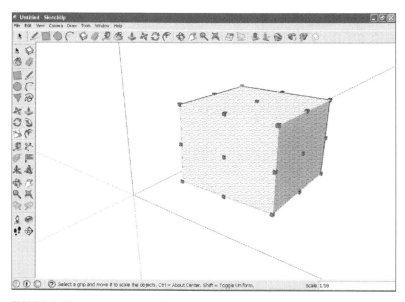

FIGURE 8.13   A newly resized cube.

> TIP: **Clicking a Cube Selects One Face for Scaling**
>
> If you don't select the whole cube before selecting the Scale tool, but simply click a cube face with the Scale tool, that face (only) is selected for resizing. See the next task for more details.

Tapering Objects in 3D

Drawing regular 3D items is nice, but what if you want to taper an object instead? What if you have a cylinder as shown in Figure 8.14?

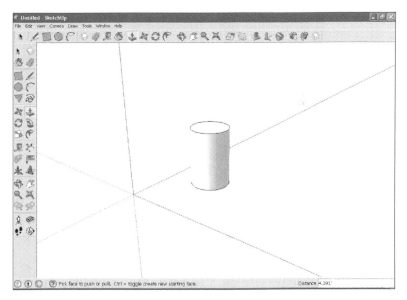

FIGURE 8.14   A cylinder.

However, you want to change the shape to be larger at the top, perhaps similar to what you see in Figure 8.15 instead. What can you do?

You can create the shape you see in Figure 8.15 using the Scale tool. Here's how it works:

1. Click the **Start Using SketchUp** button.

2. Select the **Circle tool** and draw a horizontal circle.

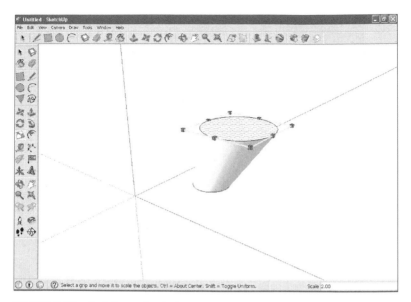

FIGURE 8.15   A deformed cylinder.

3. Select the **Push/Pull tool** in the toolbar and pull the circle up into a cylinder.

4. From the **Large Tool Set** select the **Scale tool** (open the Large Tool Set from the View menu if necessary).

5. Click the circle at the top of the cylinder. The circle has sizing handles added to it.

6. Click the mouse button on a sizing handle. The sizing handle you choose determines how the top circle of the cylinder will be stretched when you move the mouse.

7. Drag the mouse to stretch the cylinder in the direction you've chosen. The cylinder stretches as you pull it.

8. Release the mouse button. When you do, the cylinder is fixed in place at its new size, as shown in Figure 8.15.

But what if you wanted to create a regular funnel shape instead? Take a look at the next task.

Scaling from the Center of Objects

So far, we've tapered an object by pulling one edge. But to taper an object more regularly, you should taper from the center of the object. Suppose you started with the cylinder in the previous task but wanted to end up with the funnel shown in Figure 8.16.

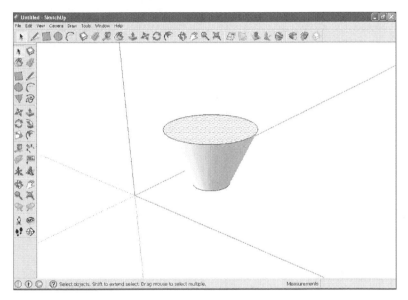

FIGURE 8.16 A funnel.

Here's how to create the funnel:

1. Click the **Start Using SketchUp** button.

2. Select the **Circle tool** and draw a horizontal circle.

3. Select the **Push/Pull tool** in the toolbar and pull the circle up into a cylinder.

4. From the **Large Tool Set** select the **Scale tool** (open the Large Tool Set from the View menu if necessary).

5. Click the circle at the top of the cylinder. The circle has sizing handles added to it.

6. Press the Ctrl key. Pressing the Ctrl key makes the Scale tool scale objects from their center, which is what we want in this case.

7. Click and hold the mouse button on a sizing handle.

8. Drag the mouse to stretch the cylinder into the funnel shape.

9. Release the mouse button. When you do, the funnel is fixed in place at its new size, as shown in Figure 8.16.

That lets you scale objects from their center.

Setting Exact Scale

What if you had an object and you wanted to expand it by exactly a factor of two? You can set the exact amount you resize an object by with the Scale tool as follows, where we're expanding a cube by a factor of two:

1. Click the **Start Using SketchUp** button.

2. Select the **Rectangle tool** and draw a horizontal rectangle.

3. Select the **Push/Pull tool** in the toolbar and pull the rectangle up into a cube.

4. Select the **Select tool** in the toolbar.

5. Draw a selection rectangle around the cube with the mouse.

6. Release the mouse button. When you do, the cube is selected.

7. From the **Large Tool Set** select the **Scale tool** (open the Large Tool Set from the View menu if necessary).

8. Press the mouse button on a sizing handle.

9. Drag the mouse to stretch the cube in the direction you want.

10. Release the mouse button.

11. Enter the factor by which you want to scale the cube. In this example, we'll scale the cube by a factor of two, so type **2**.

12. Press Enter. When you do, the cube is expanded from its original size by a factor of two.

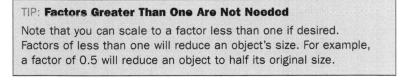

TIP: **Factors Greater Than One Are Not Needed**

Note that you can scale to a factor less than one if desired. Factors of less than one will reduce an object's size. For example, a factor of 0.5 will reduce an object to half its original size.

And that's setting exact scale.

Using the Follow-Me Tool

The Follow-Me tool lets you drag shapes down a path you specify. Take a look at the object in Figure 8.17.

The Follow-Me Tool

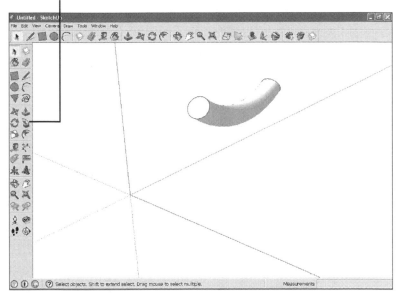

FIGURE 8.17   A curved object drawn using the Follow-Me tool.

Can you draw that in SketchUp?

You sure can. All you need to do is to draw a circle, set up a curved path, then move the circle along the curved path with the Follow-Me tool (also shown in Figure 8.17). The Follow-Me tool lets you move shapes along paths to make them 3D. Here's how creating the shape shown in Figure 8.17 works:

1. Click the **Start Using SketchUp** button.

2. Select the **Circle tool** and draw a circle like the one shown in Figure 8.18.

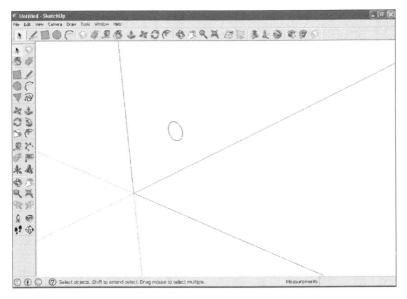

FIGURE 8.18   A circle.

3. Select the **Arc tool** in the toolbar.

4. Click the mouse in your drawing at one end of the path you want to pull the circle along.

5. Click the mouse at the other end point of the path you want to pull the circle along.

6. Pull the arc into the shape you want the circle to be pulled along to create your 3D object.

7. Select the **Select tool**.

8. Click the circle to select it.

9. Select the **Move tool**.

10. Move the circle to the end of the arc, as shown in Figure 8.19.

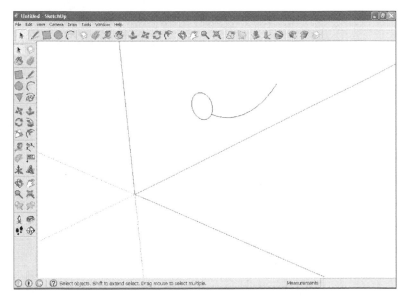

FIGURE 8.19   A circle with an arc.

11. From the **Large Tool Set** select the **Follow-Me tool** (open the Large Tool Set from the View menu if necessary).

12. Now we're ready to use the Follow-Me tool. If the circle isn't selected, select it with the **Select tool** and then select the **Follow-Me tool** again.

13. Use the mouse to drag the circle along the arc. The Follow-Me tool senses that you're following the arc and keeps the circle moving along it to draw the shape you see in Figure 8.17.

TIP: **You Don't Have to Drag the Follow-Me Tool**

You don't have to drag the Follow-Me tool along a path if you don't want to. Simply select the edges that form the path you want with the Select tool so they appear as dotted lines (and form a connected path). Then select the Follow-Me tool and click the shape you want to have the Follow-Me tool drag around the path you selected automatically.

The Follow-Me tool is invaluable if you want to create a shape by moving another shape along a certain path.

X-Raying Objects, Creating Guides and Offsets

In this lesson, we're going to extend our SketchUp skill set by x-raying objects, creating construction guides, and offsetting edges to make copies of them.

Getting Started

When you x-ray surfaces, you can see what's behind them. That's great when your model gets more involved and objects start obstructing objects and you don't want to keep rotating around to see behind them.

You can create construction guides with the Tape Measure tool. Construction guides are dotted lines that you use for reference when moving or aligning other objects, and they're great when you're laying out the parts of your model.

We'll also see how to create offsets in this lesson. An offset is a copy of an edge that you can resize just by dragging the mouse, and offsets are very useful when you're building items like doors and windows to build frames.

We'll see all this in this lesson—let's get started by giving some objects the X-ray treatment.

> NOTE: **Know Your Tools**
>
> It's assumed in these tasks that you have been progressing through each lesson in order and learning about the individual tools used here. In case you need to flip back for review, check out

> Lesson 3, "Drawing Shapes: Lines, Rectangles, Polygons, and Circles," for more on the Line, Rectangle, and Circle tools. See Lesson 5, "Going 3D," for a refresher on the Push/Pull and Move tools.

X-Raying Objects

You can "see through" objects in SketchUp, which is very powerful in a number of situations; for example, when you have two objects that obscure one another and don't want to keep rotating the drawing all the time, or when you have two objects that overlap and want to position them correctly with regard to each other.

Turning on X-ray view is easy. We'll again use the Engineering–Feet template and draw a few cubes; then we'll X-ray them to show how this works:

1. Click the **Start Using SketchUp** button.

2. Select the **Rectangle tool** and draw a horizontal rectangle.

3. Select the **Push/Pull tool** in the toolbar and pull the rectangle up into a cube.

4. Repeat steps 2 and 3 to draw another cube.

5. Select the **Select tool** in the toolbar.

6. Draw a selection box around one of the cubes to select it.

7. Select the **Move tool** in the toolbar.

8. Move the selected cube behind the other cube. You can see what this looks like in Figure 9.1.

9. From the View menu, select **Face Style**. A submenu appears.

10. Select the **X-ray** item in the submenu. This turns on X-ray viewing and makes all objects "transparent," as you can see in Figure 9.2.

Note that you can now see through the obscuring cube to the cube behind it. Very cool.

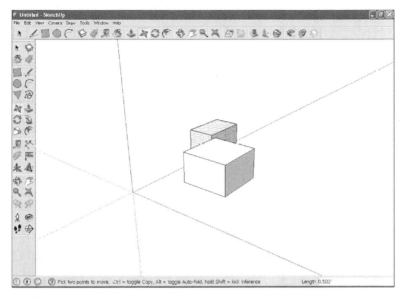

FIGURE 9.1   One cube obscures another.

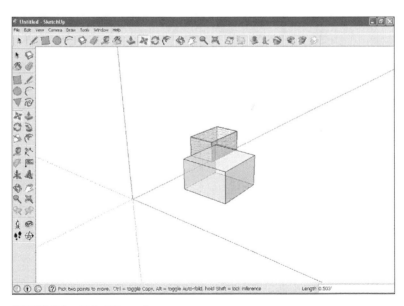

FIGURE 9.2   Using X-ray view.

As you can see, X-ray vision is a great tool to help you manage multiple objects when they start to obscure each other. To turn it off, select the View menu's Face Style item to open the submenu, and select the X-ray item again to toggle X-ray vision off.

Offsetting Edges with the Offset Tool

The Offset tool lets you create copies of edges and move them away from the original edge. That's good when you have a complex surface and want to draw a matching surface that's smaller or larger. To see this in action, we'll start in this task with the object you see in Figure 9.3.

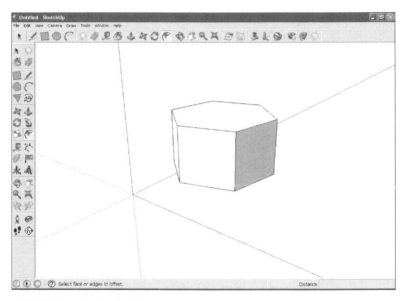

FIGURE 9.3   A 3D object.

Using the Offset tool and the Push/Pull tool, we'll change this object to the one you see in Figure 9.4 with just a couple of clicks.

The Offset Tool

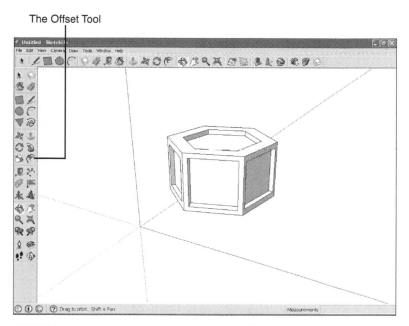

FIGURE 9.4 Decorating an object using the Offset tool.

Here's how it works:

1. Click the **Start Using SketchUp** button.

2. Select **Toolbars** from the View menu. This opens a submenu.

3. Select the submenu's **Large Tool Set** item. This opens the large toolbar.

4. Select the **Polygon tool** in the Large Tool Set toolbar.

5. Draw a horizontal pentagon. Pentagons are the default polygon drawn by the Polygon tool.

6. Select the **Push/Pull tool** in the toolbar.

7. Pull the pentagon up into 3D.

   Now we'll use the Offset tool to draw the offsets we need.

8. Select the **Offset tool** in the Large Tool Set toolbar. The Offset tool is the tool that displays an image of two concentric circle sections with a red arrow connecting them (shown in Figure 9.4).

9. Click a surface of the object. Clicking a surface tells the Offset tool which surface it should draw offsets of.

10. Move the mouse to make an offset appear. The Offset tool draws an offset following the edges of the current surface, as you can see in Figure 9.5.

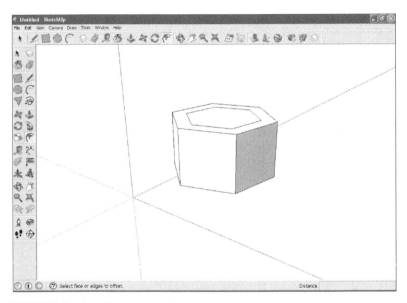

FIGURE 9.5   An offset on a surface.

11. Size the offset surface by moving the mouse.

12. Release the mouse button. This locks the offset into place.

13. Repeat steps 8–12 for all visible faces of the object. Use the **Rotation tool** if you need to get a clearer view of a face.

14. Select the **Push/Pull tool** in the toolbar.

15. Select each offset surface and push it into the object, as shown in Figure 9.4.

As you can see, offsetting surfaces is useful and easy.

Selecting Edges to Offset

In the previous task, we offset surfaces with the Offset tool. But sometimes, you don't want to offset a whole surface—you just want to offset selected edges.

To see what that means, take a look at the door in Figure 9.6.

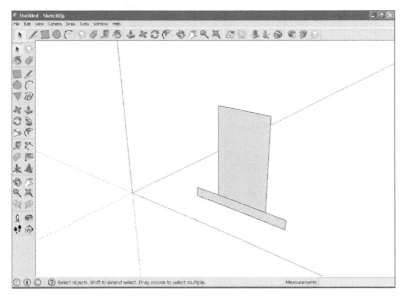

FIGURE 9.6   A door.

Now suppose that you'd like to draw a frame around the door. Using the Offset tool to offset the door's surface leads to trouble, however, because the frame the Offset tool is drawing overlaps the lintel (the board at the bottom of a door), as you can see in Figure 9.7.

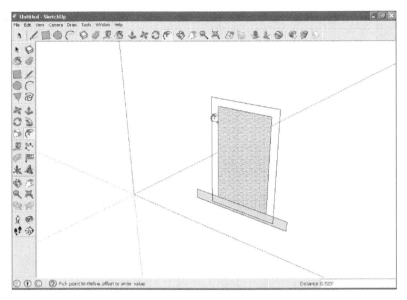

FIGURE 9.7   An offset overlapping the lintel.

Wouldn't it be nice if you could just offset the top three edges of the door, as shown in Figure 9.8?

That way, you could use the Offset tool to draw the door frame without having the frame overlap the door's lintel.

You can do this if you use the Offset tool with edges, not surfaces. Here's how it works:

1. Click the **Start Using SketchUp** button.

2. Select the **Line tool** in the Getting Started toolbar.

3. Draw the door and lintel as shown in Figure 9.6.

4. Select the **Select tool** in the toolbar.

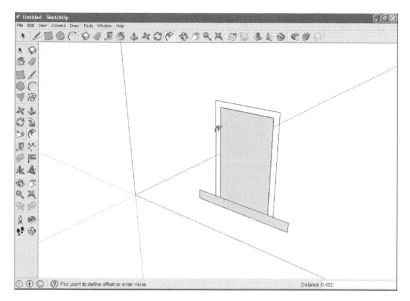

FIGURE 9.8   An offset using edges.

5. Hold down the **Ctrl** key (Option key on the Mac) and click the three upper edges of the door. Holding down the Ctrl (or Option) key means you can make multiple selections just by clicking them with the Select tool.

When you're done, the top three edges of the door should be selected.

6. From the Large Tool Set select the **Offset tool** (open the Large Tool Set from the View menu if necessary).

7. Click inside the door.

8. Move the mouse to make an offset appear. The Offset tool draws an offset following the edges of the current surface, as you can see in Figure 9.8.

9. Size the offset surface by moving the mouse.

10. Release the mouse button. This locks the offset into place, as you can see in Figure 9.9.

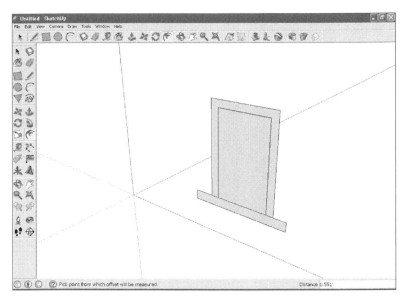

FIGURE 9.9   A new door frame.

As you can see, offsetting surfaces is easy.

Creating Exact Offsets

Because this is SketchUp, you might assume you can create measured offsets of exactly a precise length offset from the surrounding edges—and you'd be right.

Suppose, for example, that you draw a cube and want a surface drawn on one face offset from the surrounding edges by exactly one foot. Can you do it? Yes, you can; just follow these steps:

1. Click the **Start Using SketchUp** button.

2. Select the **Rectangle tool** and draw a horizontal rectangle.

3. Select the **Push/Pull tool** in the toolbar and pull the rectangle up into a cube.

4. From the Large Tool Set select the **Offset tool** (open the Large Tool Set from the View menu if necessary).

5. Click the surface you want to create the offset on. The surface becomes selected when you click it.

6. Enter the size of the offset you want. In this example, we'll create a one-foot offset. In general, you enter a length and then the units—you can use these units:

   ▶ **cm** to signify centimeters

   ▶ **m** to signify meters

   ▶ ' for feet

   ▶ " for inches

   Thus, for example, 1' means one foot, so type '.

7. Press **Enter**. The offset appears, as you see in Figure 9.10.

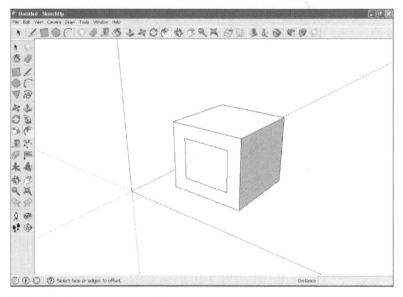

FIGURE 9.10   A measured offset.

That's the way to measure offsets.

Repeating Offsets on Other Surfaces

You can repeat offsets on different surfaces with the click of the mouse. Here's how it works; in this example, we'll repeat offsets on various faces of a cube:

1. Click the **Start Using SketchUp** button.

2. Select the **Rectangle tool** and draw a horizontal rectangle.

3. Select the **Push/Pull tool** in the toolbar and pull the rectangle up into a cube.

4. From the Large Tool Set select the **Offset tool** (open the Large Tool Set from the View menu if necessary).

5. Draw an offset edge on one surface of the cube. You can see an example in Figure 9.11.

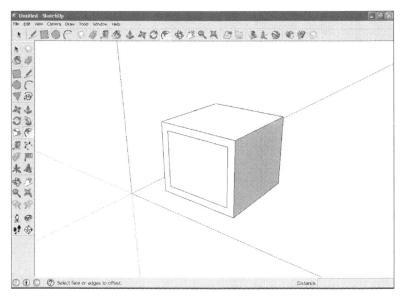

FIGURE 9.11 An offset edge.

6. Double-click the mouse on another surface of the cube. Double-clicking the mouse draws another offset at the same distance you drew the previous one, as you see in Figure 9.12.

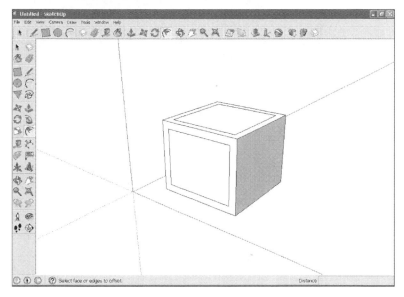

FIGURE 9.12   A new offset edge.

NOTE: **Offsets Within Offsets**

Note that you can create offsets within offsets using the same distance as well—for example, see Figure 9.13, where we've clicked inside the first offset rectangle.

Creating offsets that are all the same size is extremely useful when you have, say, multiple panels you want to create in a drawing.

Measuring Distances with the Tape Measure

The Tape Measure tool lets you measure distances handily in your model. When you're drawing plans to scale, that can be indispensable.

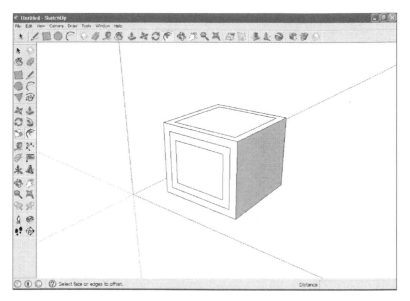

FIGURE 9.13   An offset inside an offset.

In this example, we'll draw a cube and then measure one face. Here's how it works:

1. Click the **Start Using SketchUp** button.

2. Select the **Rectangle tool** and draw a horizontal rectangle.

3. Select the **Push/Pull tool** in the toolbar and pull the rectangle up into a cube.

4. Select the **Tape Measure tool** in the Getting Started toolbar (shown in Figure 9.14).

5. Click the mouse button on one edge of the cube. This anchors the Tape Measure tool to the location you've clicked.

6. Move the mouse to the opposite edge of the cube. You can see this at work in Figure 9.14.

You can see the width of the cube face in two places in Figure 9.14—in a ToolTip at the location of the Tape Measure tool (which reads 7.473') and in the Value Control Box, or VCB, at the lower right in SketchUp.

The Tape Measure Tool

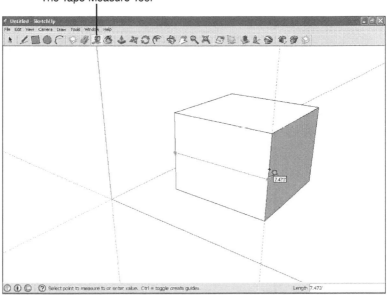

FIGURE 9.14   Using the Tape Measure tool.

TIP: **Measurements Are Always Available**

Note that the measurement in the ToolTip disappears after a moment, but the measurement is always displayed in the Value Control Box.

That's the way you can measure distances in SketchUp using the Tape Measure tool and the Value Control Box.

TIP: **Canceling the Tape Measure Tool**

After you press the mouse button and begin moving the Tape Measure tool around your drawing, it'll keep measuring distances no matter where you move the mouse. That's great if you have multiple distances to measure, but eventually you'll want to turn off the Tape Measure tool. To turn it off, select another tool, or press the Esc key.

Creating Guides with the Tape Measure Tool

Guides are dotted lines that you can use to align objects. They're very handy when you are creating a drawing with multiple objects that have to be in a specific relation to the others, such as in perfect rows. All you have to do is to align the edges of the object with the guides you've drawn from other objects.

We'll take a look at how this works by aligning three cubes in a row using guides. Here's how it works:

1. Click the **Start Using SketchUp** button.

2. Select the **Rectangle tool** and draw a horizontal rectangle.

3. Select the **Push/Pull tool** in the toolbar and pull the rectangle up into a cube.

4. Select the **Select tool** in the toolbar.

5. Draw a selection rectangle around the cube.

6. Select **Copy** from the Edit menu.

7. Select **Paste** from the Edit menu.

8. Click the mouse at the location where you want a new cube to appear.

9. Repeat steps 4–8 to create a third cube. Now you have three cubes, as shown in Figure 9.15.

10. Select the **Tape Measure tool** in the Getting Started toolbar.

11. Click the top-front edge of one of the cubes. A guide appears (represented by a dotted line), as shown in Figure 9.16.

12. Select the **Select tool** in the toolbar.

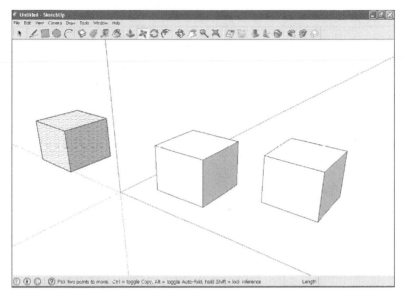

FIGURE 9.15 Three cubes.

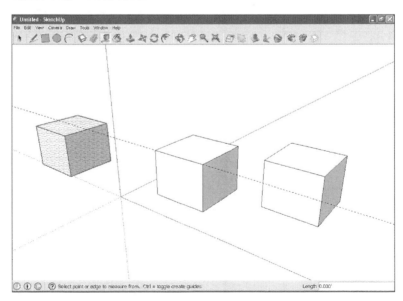

FIGURE 9.16 A new guide.

13. Draw a selection rectangle around a cube that doesn't have the guide attached.

14. Select the **Move tool** in the toolbar.

15. Move the cube into alignment with the guide, as shown in Figure 9.17.

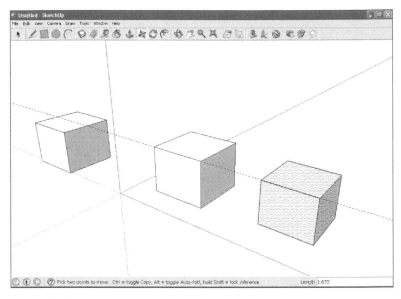

FIGURE 9.17   Aligning a cube.

16. Repeat steps 12–15 to align the third cube, as shown in Figure 9.18.

Now the three cubes are in a row, and you know how to use guides to align objects in SketchUp.

Drawing Guides at Specific Offsets

In the previous task, we added a guide to a drawing with three cubes to align those cubes in a row. But what if you also wanted to space those cubes apart at an exact distance?

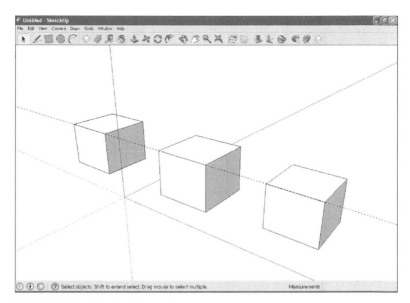

FIGURE 9.18   Aligning three cubes.

We'll see how to use guides to do that in this task. If you haven't already completed the previous task, do so now in preparation for this task.

So how do you draw guides at a specific distance away from an edge? Here's how you do it, using the three cubes example developed in the previous task:

1. Start with the three cubes aligned in a row from the previous task.

2. Select the **Tape Measure tool** in the Getting Started toolbar.

3. Click the top-right edge of the middle cube. This anchors the Tape Measure tool.

4. Move the mouse away from the middle cube toward the cube on the right. This pulls a guide out from and parallel to the top-right edge of the middle cube.

    You can pull the guide to any distance you want. In this task, we'll see how to pull it out exactly three feet.

5. Release the mouse button.

6. Enter the offset you want for the guide. In this example, we'll create a three-foot offset for the guide. In general, you enter a length and then the units. You can use these units:

▶ **cm** to signify centimeters

▶ **m** to signify meters

▶ **'** for feet

▶ **"** for inches

For example, 3' means three feet, so type **3'**.

7. Press **Enter**. The guide snaps to three feet from the middle cube, as you see in Figure 9.19.

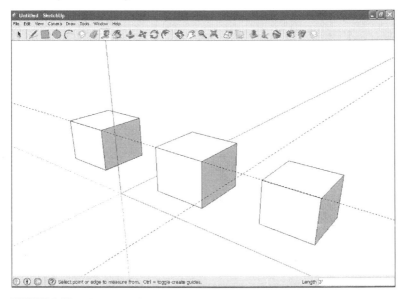

FIGURE 9.19   A new guide.

8. Select the **Select tool** in the toolbar.

9. Draw a selection rectangle around a cube that doesn't have the guide attached.

10. Select the **Move tool** in the toolbar.

11. Move the cube into alignment with the new guide, spacing it at three feet from the middle cube.

12. Select the **Tape Measure tool** in the Getting Started toolbar.

13. Click the top-left edge of the middle cube. This anchors the Tape Measure tool.

14. Move the mouse away from the middle cube toward the cube on the left.

15. Enter the offset you want for the guide. In this example, we'll create a three-foot offset for the guide, so type **3'**.

16. Press **Enter**.

17. Repeat steps 8–11 to move the left cube into alignment.

Now your cubes are in a row, and evenly spaced, as you see in Figure 9.20.

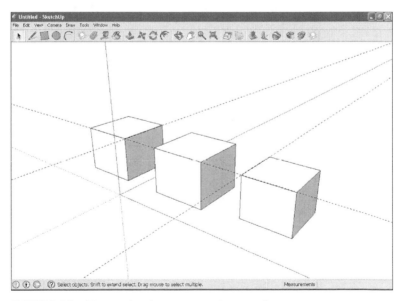

FIGURE 9.20   Three cubes in a row, evenly spaced.

Now that you've got your three cubes in a row and evenly spaced, you don't need the guides any more. How do you get rid of them? See the next task.

Deleting Guides

In the previous two tasks, you created a number of guides that you used to align three cubes. Now that the guides have served their purpose, can you get rid of them?

Yes, you can. Just follow these steps:

1. Start with the three cubes aligned in a row from the previous task.

2. Select the **Eraser tool** in the Getting Started toolbar.

3. Click and hold down the mouse button and drag the mouse over the guides in the drawing. When you do, the guides are erased, as you see in Figure 9.21.

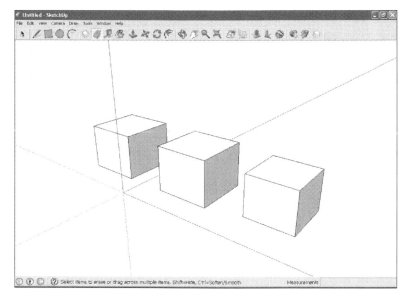

FIGURE 9.21   Erasing guides.

That's it—the guides are gone, and your cubes are all in a row.

LESSON 10

Dimensioning, Drawing Angles, and Getting Cross Sections of Models

In this lesson, we're going to take a look at three important SketchUp tools—the Dimensioning tool, the Protractor tool, and the Sectioning tool.

The Dimensioning tool lets you display dimensions in your model, as you can see in Figure 10.1.

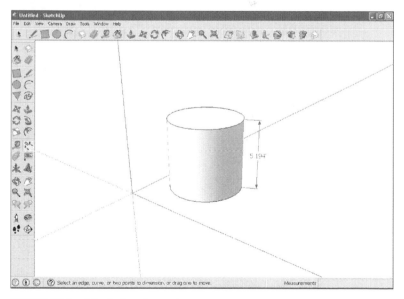

FIGURE 10.1 Displaying dimensions.

The Dimensioning tool is a great one when you're creating plans of any sort, such as architectural plans, and need to indicate distances.

The Protractor tool lets you do for angles what the Tape Measure tool (see Lesson 9, "X-Raying Objects, Creating Guides and Offsets") lets you do for straight edges. You use the Protractor to measure angles or to create guides at specific angles. That's useful if you have objects in your drawing that need to be at a certain angle from other objects, such as the slope of a roof with respect to the rest of the house.

Finally, we'll take a look at the Sectioning tool. This tool lets you create cutaway sections in your models. This way, complex models can be made clearer by taking sections of the model and making the rest of the model invisible.

All this is coming up in this lesson.

Dimensioning Distances

The Dimensioning tool lets you add dimension labels to a drawing to indicate distances. That's particularly useful when you're drawing plans where measurements are important, such as architectural plans that will be used in actual construction.

For the tasks in this lesson we'll again use the Engineering–Feet template we've used previously.

Here's how to use the Dimensioning tool to measure a cube:

1. Click the **Start Using SketchUp** button.

2. Select the **Rectangle tool** and draw a horizontal rectangle.

3. Select the **Push/Pull tool** in the toolbar and pull the rectangle up into a cube.

4. Select **Toolbars** from the View menu. This opens a submenu.

5. Select the submenu's **Large Tool Set** item. This opens the large toolbar.

6. Select the **Dimensioning tool** in the toolbar (shown in Figure 10.2).

The Dimensioning Tool

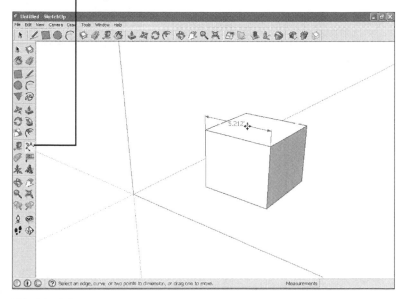

FIGURE 10.2   Pulling a dimensioning label using the Dimensioning tool.

7. Click an edge of the cube.

8. Pull a dimensioning label away from the edge. You can see what this looks like in Figure 10.2.

9. Click to fix the dimensioning label in place.

10. Repeat steps 7 and 8 for additional edges of the cube. You can see the results in Figure 10.3.

Great—now you can add dimension labels to your models.

TIP: **Dimensioning Between Any Two Points**

You can also add a dimension label between any two points in a drawing, not just an edge. To do that, select the Dimensioning tool, click the first point, and then click the second point.

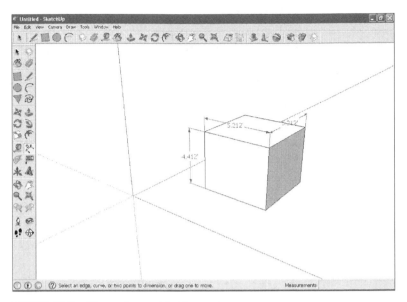

FIGURE 10.3   Dimensions added to a cube.

Dimensioning Arcs

The Dimensioning tool also lets you add dimension labels to arcs, not just straight edges. Follow these steps:

1. Click the **Start Using SketchUp** button.

2. Select the **Arc tool**.

3. Draw an arc.

4. From the **Large Tool Set** select the **Dimensioning tool** (open the Large Tool Set from the View menu if necessary).

5. Click the arc. The Dimensioning tool displays the radius of the arc, prefixed by the letter R.

6. Click the center of the arc to fix the dimension label in place. You can see what this looks like in Figure 10.4.

That's it—now you can add dimensioning labels to an arc.

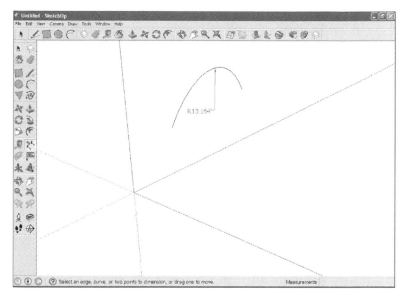

FIGURE 10.4 Dimensioning an arc.

Freezing Dimensions

When you resize an object that has a dimensioning label attached to it, the label is updated with the new length by default. However, you can lock the dimension label's displayed length so that it won't change no matter how much you resize the object. Here's how:

1. Click the **Start Using SketchUp** button.

2. Select the **Rectangle tool** and draw a horizontal rectangle.

3. Select the **Push/Pull tool** in the toolbar and pull the rectangle up into a cube.

4. From the **Large Tool Set** select the **Dimensioning tool** (open the Large Tool Set from the View menu if necessary).

5. Click an edge of the cube.

6. Pull a dimensioning guide away from the edge to create a dimensioning label.

7. Click to fix the dimensioning guide in place. The dimensioning label displays the length of the edge you've attached it to, as shown in Figure 10.5.

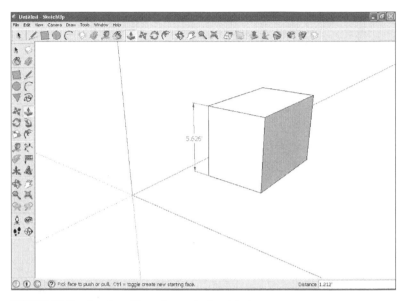

FIGURE 10.5   A cube with a dimensioning label.

8. Select the **Push/Pull tool** in the toolbar.

9. Pull the cube up vertically as you see in Figure 10.6. Note that the length measurement in the dimensioning label changes to match the new height.

10. Double-click the dimensioning label.

11. Enter a new length for the dimension. In this example, we'll create a six-foot length. In general, you enter a length and then the units—you can use these units:

- ▶ **cm** to signify centimeters
- ▶ **m** to signify meters
- ▶ **'** for feet
- ▶ **"** for inches

For example, 6' means six feet, so you would type **6'**.

Now the dimension label reads six feet, as you can see in Figure 10.7, and it won't change no matter how you resize the object.

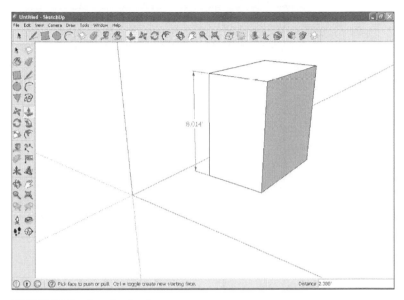

FIGURE 10.6 A resized cube.

Setting your own dimensions can be very useful when you're creating architectural or other plans.

Configuring Dimensioning Labels

You've seen the default font and style for dimensioning labels in the previous tasks and you might not like it. Fortunately, you can change it.

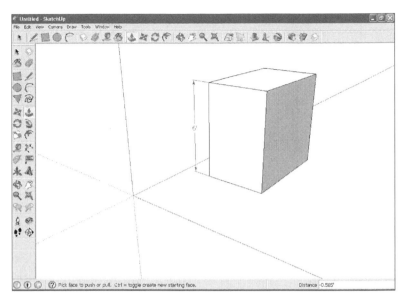

FIGURE 10.7   A fixed dimension.

For example, in this task, we'll change the font used for dimensioning labels from the default Tahoma 12 points to Times New Roman 18 points (or another font and font size that your system supports):

1. Click the **Start Using SketchUp** button.

2. Select the **Rectangle tool** and draw a horizontal rectangle.

3. Select the **Push/Pull tool** in the toolbar and pull the rectangle up into a cube.

4. From the **Large Tool Set** select the **Dimensioning tool** (open the Large Tool Set from the View menu if necessary).

5. Click an edge of the cube.

6. Pull a dimensioning label away from the edge.

7. Click to fix the dimensioning label in place.

8. Select **Model Info** from the Window menu. This opens the Model Info dialog box.

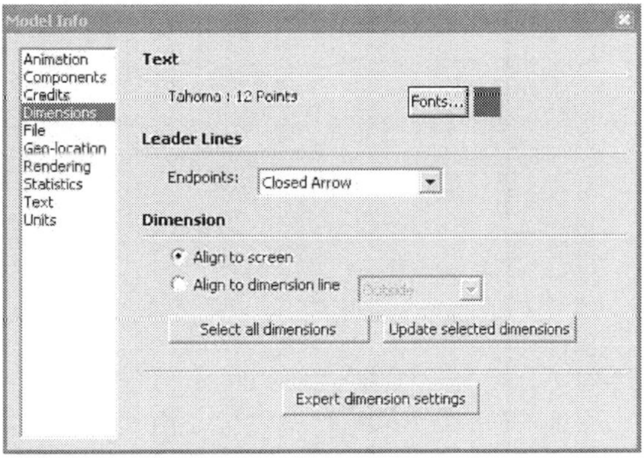

FIGURE 10.8 The Dimensions settings dialog.

9. Click the **Dimensions** item at the left in the Model Info dialog box. This opens the Dimensions settings, as you see in Figure 10.8.

10. Click the **Select All Dimensions** button.

11. Click the **Font** button. This opens the Font dialog box, as you see in Figure 10.9.

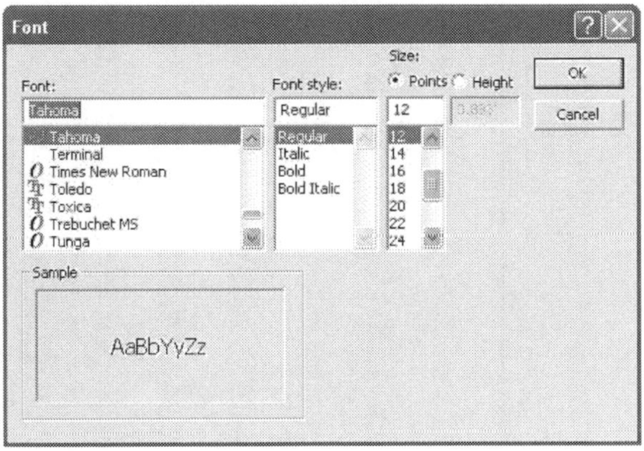

FIGURE 10.9 The Font dialog box.

12. Select the **Times New Roman** font (or another font supported by your system).

13. Select **18** point font size.

14. Click **OK**.

15. Click the **Update Selected Dimensions** button.

16. Click the **X** button at the upper right in the Model Info dialog box to close it. The font in your dimensioning labels changes to match your new settings.

> TIP: **Setting Arrow Styles**
>
> Note that you can also set the style for arrows used in dimensioning labels. Just select the new style you want from the drop-down list in the Model Info dialog box–closed arrows (that is, filled-in arrow heads), open arrows, dotted lines, and more.

And that lets you configure dimension labels.

Measuring Angles

The Protractor tool is great for measuring angles. Suppose you had the object with an angle on one side, as you see in Figure 10.10. Now suppose that you wanted to measure that angle. How could you do it?

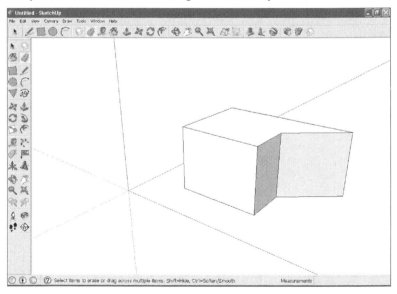

FIGURE 10.10 An object with an angle in one face.

You could use the Protractor tool. This tool is to angles what the Tape Measure tool is to lengths—that is, you can measure angles with it.

To see how this works, follow these steps:

1. Click the **Start Using SketchUp** button.

2. Select the **Rectangle tool** and draw a horizontal rectangle.

3. Select the **Push/Pull tool** in the toolbar and pull the rectangle up into a cube.

4. Select the **Line tool** in the toolbar.

5. Draw a vertical line on the right face of the cube.

6. Select the **Move tool** in the toolbar.

7. Pull the right-most edge of the cube out until your object looks like Figure 10.11.

The Protractor Tool

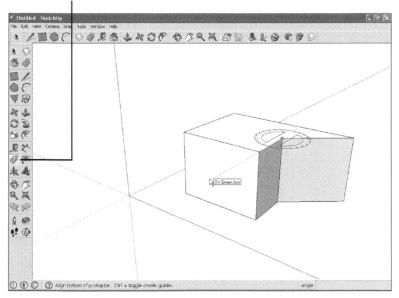

FIGURE 10.11 The Protractor tool in use.

8. Select the View menu's **Toolbars** item. This opens a submenu.

9. Select the submenu's **Large Tool Set** item. This opens the large toolbar.

10. Select the **Protractor tool** in the toolbar.

11. Click the vertex of the angle you plan to measure. A protractor appears at the location you've clicked, as shown in Figure 10.11.

12. Click one of the edges that make up the angle.

13. Click the other edge that makes up the angle. Two dotted lines extend from the protractor, measuring the angle, as you see in Figure 10.12.

You can see the angle the protractor is measuring in the Value Control Box at the lower right: 128.6 degrees.

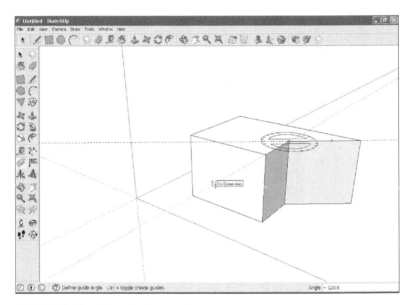

FIGURE 10.12   Measuring an angle.

That's great if you need to measure an angle, but what if you want to specify a certain angle instead, and set up guides to match?

Take a look at the next task.

Creating Guides at Specific Angles

You can also create guides at given angles. Take a look at the two cubes in Figure 10.13.

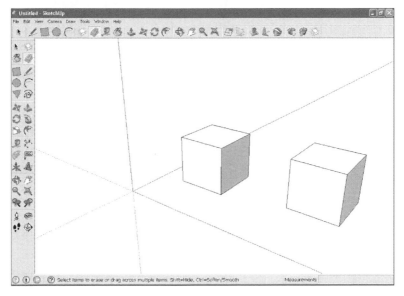

FIGURE 10.13 Two cubes in a drawing.

Suppose you need them to be aligned so that the back face of the right cube is at 145° with respect to the right face of the left cube, as shown in Figure 10.14. How could you move the cubes to meet this criteria?

You use the Protractor tool to draw construction guides at an angle. Here's how it works:

1. Click the **Start Using SketchUp** button.

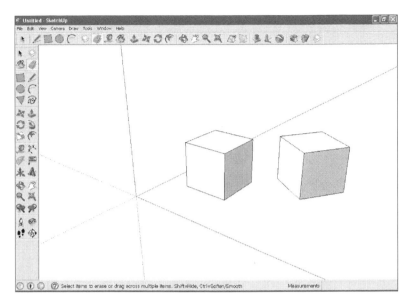

FIGURE 10.14   Two cubes at a specified angle.

2. Select the **Rectangle tool** and draw a horizontal rectangle.

3. Select the **Push/Pull tool** in the toolbar and pull the rectangle up into a cube.

4. Select the **Select tool** in the toolbar.

5. Draw a selection rectangle around the cube.

6. Select the Edit menu's **Copy** item.

7. Select the Edit menu's **Paste** item.

8. Click the mouse at the location where you want a new cube to appear.

9. From the **Large Tool Set** select the **Protractor tool** (open the Large Tool Set from the View menu if necessary).

10. Click the upper-left corner of the left cube. A protractor appears at the location you've clicked, as shown in Figure 10.15.

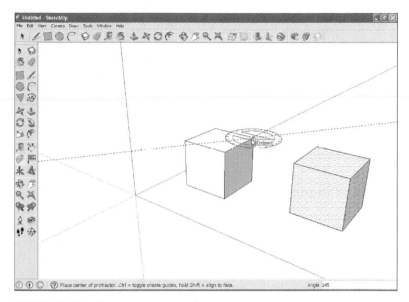

FIGURE 10.15   A protractor on a cube.

11. Click the top left edge of the left cube.

12. Move the mouse in the direction you want your angle guide to appear.

13. Type in the angle at which you want the guide to appear. In this example, we'll use 145 degrees, so type in **145**.

14. Press **Enter**.

An angle guide snaps into position, as you can see in Figure 10.15.

15. Use the Move and Rotate tools to move the right cube into position along the guide, as shown in Figure 10.16.

16. Use the Eraser tool to delete the guide. You end up with the drawing previously shown in Figure 10.14.

Now you're able to draw construction guides not only along straight edges, but also along angles.

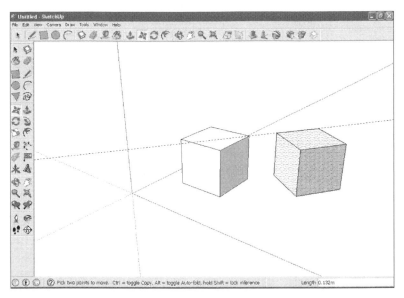

FIGURE 10.16   Aligning a cube.

> TIP: **Drawing Roof Slopes**
>
> If you want to draw a roof slope, measured as two numbers sepa-
> rated by a colon, you can enter that instead of an angle in degrees.
> For example, you might enter 6:12 and then press the Enter key.

Creating Cutaway Views of Your Model

SketchUp enables you to get cutaway views of your models. Suppose you
had a model of a motorcycle, as shown in Figure 10.17.

As with any complex model, you might want to display various cross sections to indicate what makes the model tick. You can do that with the
Section Pane tool.

Just follow these steps:

   1. Click the **Start Using SketchUp** button.

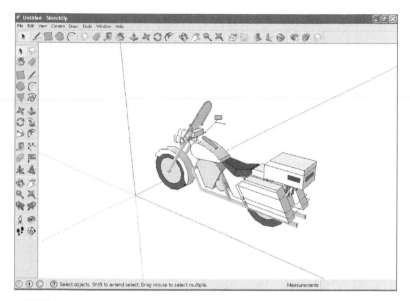

FIGURE 10.17   A motorcycle.

2. Draw your model.

3. Select the **View** menu's **Toolbars** item. This opens a submenu.

4. Select the submenu's **Large Tool Set** item. This opens the large toolbar.

5. Select the **Section Pane tool** in the toolbar (shown in Figure 10.18).

6. Move the Section Pane tool over your model. The Section Pane tool draws a plane that aligns with any underlying surface.

7. Click when you've selected the right cutaway section with the Section Pane tool. You can see an example in Figure 10.18.

Want to preserve the part of the model that was cut and cut the rest instead? See the next task.

The Section Pane Tool

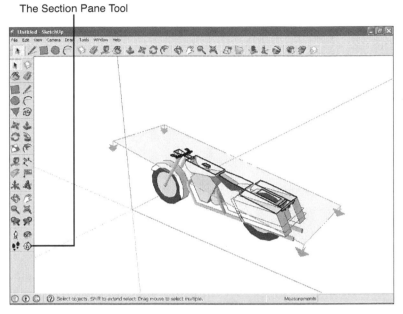

FIGURE 10.18   A cross section using the Section Pane tool.

Reversing the Direction of a Section Cut

By default, the Section Pane tool cuts away the top of a model. But you can make it cut away the bottom of a model instead.

Just follow these steps:

1. Click the **Start Using SketchUp** button.

2. Draw your model.

3. From the **Large Tool Set** select the **Section Pane tool** (open the Large Tool Set from the View menu if necessary).

4. Move the Section Pane tool over your model. The Section Pane tool draws a plane that aligns with any underlying surface.

5. Click when you've selected the right cutaway section with the Section Pane tool.

6. Right click the section pane. A context menu appears.

7. Select the **Reverse** item in the context menu. The part of the model that was cut away reappears, and the part that was visible disappears, as you can see in the example in Figure 10.19.

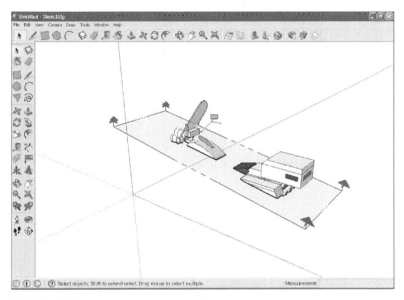

FIGURE 10.19   Reversing a cross section.

Now you've got complete control over section panes.

Index

2D objects
3D objects
    drawing, subtracting elements method, 115-117
    scaling, 172-175
    tapering, 175-176
    text, drawing, 91-93
3D Text tool, 91-93
3D Warehouse, 136-138

A

acute angles, rounding, 76-79
aligning objects with guides, 198-201
angles
    construction guides, creating, 217-220
    of guides, setting, 217-220
    measuring, 214-216
annotating objects with text, 86-88
Arc tool, 75
arcs
    dimensioning, 208
    drawing, 73-75
    multiple tangent arcs, drawing, 79-80
    number of segments, setting, 80-81
    tangent to corners, drawing, 76-79
automatic shading, eliminating, 146-147
axes, 44-45

C

canceling operations, 160
Circle tool, 62-64
circles
    drawing, 62-64
    number of sides, setting, 67-69
collections, 18-19
    texture collections, 145-146
component libraries, 18-19
Component Sampler, 135-136
components, 129-130
    3D Warehouse, 136-138
    comparing to groups, 129-130
    creating, 125-127

U

X

Y

Z

FREE Online Edition

Your purchase of **Sams Teach Yourself Google SketchUp 8 in 10 Minutes** includes access to a free online edition for 45 days through the Safari Books Online subscription service. Nearly every Sams book is available online through Safari Books Online, along with more than 5,000 other technical books and videos from publishers such as Addison-Wesley Professional, Cisco Press, Exam Cram, IBM Press, O'Reilly, Prentice Hall, and Que.

SAFARI BOOKS ONLINE allows you to search for a specific answer, cut and paste code, download chapters, and stay current with emerging technologies.

Activate your FREE Online Edition at
www.informit.com/safarifree

> **STEP 1:** Enter the coupon code: OQUNHAA.

> **STEP 2:** New Safari users, complete the brief registration form. Safari subscribers, just log in.

If you have difficulty registering on Safari or accessing the online edition, please e-mail customer-service@safaribooksonline.com

Addison Wesley   AdobePress   ALPHA   Cisco Press   Press   IBM Press   lynda.com   Microsoft Press   New Riders

O'REILLY   Peachpit Press   PRENTICE HALL   QUE   RedBooks   SAMS   SAS   Sun   WILEY